# PAINFUL AFFAIRS

## Looking For Love Through Addiction And Co-dependency

JOSEPH R. CRUSE, M.D.

Health Communications, Inc.
Deerfield Beach, Florida

Joseph R. Cruse, M.D.
ONSITE Training & Consulting, Inc.
2820 West Main
Rapid City, South Dakota 57702

**Library of Congress Cataloging-in-Publication Data**

Cruse, Joseph R., 1930-
Painful affairs: looking for love through addiction and Co-dependency / Joseph R. Cruse.
p. cm.
Bibliography: p.
ISBN 1-55874-026-0
1. Substance abuse — Psychological aspects. 2. Co-dependence (Psychology) I. Title.
RC564.C78 1989 89-1845
616.86'001'9 — dc19 CIP


ISBN 1-55874-026-0



Published by: Health Communications, Inc.
3201 S.W. 15th Street
Deerfield Beach, Florida 33442

*Cover Design: Reta Thomas*
*Airbrush Illustration: Iris Slones*

# DEDICATION

In *Smithsonian Magazine* Margaret Woolfolk states that "dedications are written last and read first" and are "the writer's opportunity to pay a debt, show appreciation or reward the person who put up with the most aggravation throughout the project — usually a spouse." I need to do all three of the above.

This book is divided into two major parts plus a prologue (my chemical dependency story) and an epilogue (my co-dependency story).

I wish to pay a debt of omission by dedicating Part I, Chemical Dependency, to my children. Part I is a study of a disease that I have. I need to express my gratitude to them for their patience, faith in me, their loyalty and their love for me during the erratic and confusing years that I was in the throes of active chemical dependency. I love you, Todd, Don and Jolene.

I wish to show my appreciation to those many men and women members of 12-Step support groups who have helped me into recovery from chemical dependency and co-dependency. I need to publicly express appreciation and love especially to Del and Meribell Sharbutt, Paul and Maxine Ohliger and the Onsite Reconstruction Family.

Part II, Co-dependency, is dedicated to my spouse, to show my deep, deep appreciation for her "putting up with the aggravations throughout this project." More importantly, I am grateful to God for giving to her such clarity, conviction and commitment toward the recovery of this disease. She has patience and love for me, both as an author and a recovering co-dependent that is endless . . . just the amount I needed . . . I love you, Sharon.

Easter, 1989

# CONTENTS

# FOREWORD

### By David Smith, M.D.

Joe Cruse is an old friend and valued colleague. His book, *Painful Affairs: Looking for Love Through Addiction and Co-dependency,* is a unique blend of his own recovery, his teaching model of chemical dependency and his innovative theory of co-dependency.

Joe is a major figure in the field of chemical dependency and has made many contributions to addiction medicine. His own recovery has served as both inspiration and role model for chemically dependent physicians struggling to take the first step.

In addition to his work in helping others, Joe has evolved a teaching and staging model in describing chemical dependency that includes a toxic agent, a susceptible host and a permissive environment. The interplay of these three variables not only describes chemical dependency, but allows us to *assess* the potential risk for developing the disease of addiction.

This book describes the early love affair with a chemical that exists in the first stages of chemical dependency, followed by self-medication and the toxic signs and symptoms as addictive disease progresses. The stages and severity of chemical dependency are outlined with the associated physical, social and spiritual complications resulting from drug-induced biochemical disorders of the brain.

Joe, in association with his wife Sharon Wegscheider-Cruse, has expanded the field of chemical dependency to better understand addiction as a family disease, incorporating innovative concepts of addiction and co-dependency. He demonstrates that co-dependency signs and symptoms of denial, emotional suppression and compulsive behavior are accompanied by complications remarkably similar to those of chemical dependency.

Parallel with these two important clinical areas, Joe describes his own story in both chemical dependency and co-dependency, giving a dramatic reality to the information contained in this book.

Joe's recovery, his model for chemical dependency, and his approach to co-dependency are inspiring and important subjects. His book takes on the difficult and challenging task of integrating all three so that we may better understand the difficult processes of addiction, co-dependency and recovery.

PROLOGUE

# My Chemical Dependency Story

Little kids have troubles, so do bigger kids and certainly adults. I could hardly stand some of the little kid pain from my little kid troubles. I suffered until I was 18 years old and then . . . I found it . . . alcohol. I immediately fell head over heels in love with it. Relief and reward came with it! I found it!

Before I began to drink, when my feelings of being a phony were greatest, if I had known then how to get drunk, I would have. When I used to cheat at games or when I threw a croquet mallet through our only big bay window or bounced a muddy tennis ball against the house time and time again and was caught . . . if I would have known how to get drunk, I would have. Or when my high school girlfriend gave me back my letter jacket or when I wasn't elected to a class office . . . I would have got drunk if I would have known how. When I spotted my dad at my only junior league ball game he had ever gone to, I tried to steal second base with two outs and the ball in the pitcher's hand, ending our season. If I would have known how, I would have got drunk over that. Small matters to a large adult, large matters to a small boy.

I had many heroes — Steve Canyon, Tarzan, Terry of *Terry And The Pirates.* I didn't like reading *Orphan Annie,* she was always alone. That scared me. I didn't like *Alice in Wonderland* because she fell into the dark underground and was around some very strange people. That scared me, too. I didn't like any story, movie or cartoon where young children were out in the world on their own. That scared me. I received comforting feelings of security from the size of adults. If they were big, they could certainly protect us.

I developed a process of sitting and waiting, watching and waiting, trying hard to see if someone would notice me. When I wasn't noticed, that seemed normal. I decided to just wait. So much of my life was just sitting and waiting — sitting at the foot of my dad's chair while he read the paper and had his drinks, waiting to be noticed. Waiting for hair to grow on my chest, waiting for physical strength and courage, waiting for the sign or message as to what I was really supposed to do in life.

All of this waiting wouldn't have been so bad, except that the entire time that I waited, I felt lonely and yearning, not even knowing what I was yearning for.

As a senior in high school at a church camp, I had "witnessed" and consecrated my life to God, not even knowing what all that meant. I then went out and got drunk for 25 years until the age of 43. My drinking was moderate in college, became much heavier in medical school and was extremely heavy during my internship, especially on weekends. I left the military after nine years of service, having been able to work myself up to a significant position at a large teaching hospital in Washington, D.C.

I left the service with a flask in one hand and grandiose floorplans and slides for a "Family Live-in Cancer Hospital" in the other hand. I decided to build a specialized medical center in California. I wandered up and down Wilshire Boulevard in Los Angeles to raise money . . . frustrated all day and drunk all night. I was totally unsuccessful. I had to go to work, so I set up practice in Palm Springs, California.

Controlled drinking is a skill of the alcoholic, and for seven years I demonstrated this skill admirably, while my practice was growing. Weekends and out-of-town trips were filled with heavy drinking episodes. Three years before I began my actual recovery, I was taken to Alcoholics Anonymous but I continued to run my own program. I called myself a "sipping slipper," having only two cans of Club Cocktails each evening on the way home. I did this for 14 months, a prime example of an alcoholic's controlled drinking. At least I had my ten minutes of buzz and my own cocktail hour with myself. But I was lonely . . . and I waited.

I tried antabuse and even combined it with a teaspoon of bourbon. The antabuse reaction of severe flushing, rapid heartbeats and panting was better than sitting alone and yearning, even if it only lasted 15 to 20 minutes. I began to look forward to my antabuse reactions each evening. I beeped myself out of self-help groups with my beeper, drove around alone . . . and waited.

I tried a long and lonely month at a nationally recognized treatment center. It had its impact on me, but not immediately. I went out and began using pills in order to stay away from alcohol. I became my own physician and pharmacist. This whole time I felt alone and yearning for *something*. My yearning went on and on. Even in my own family I felt alone. Many events began to occur. I now realize that when I was hospitalized, my own attending physicians didn't know what to do with me, so how in the world could I?

Denial is a major obstacle to the treatment of the alcoholic, especially the alcoholic physician. In my mind there are three kinds of denial that allowed me to prolong my excessive drinking and get into trouble with it:

***Denial by my colleagues, by society and by myself.***

## Colleague Denial

My experience shows that physicians do not like nor know how nor want to make a diagnosis of alcoholism in a colleague. I was admitted to a hospital five times with problems that were a direct result of alcoholism, but alcoholism was never mentioned. This was due in part to a lack of knowledge, to a good-intentioned desire to "cover-up" and to the fear of legal embarrassment and/or confrontation. It could be said that these attending physicians were unknowing, unwitting and unwilling.

At age 27 I was admitted to the hospital with a diagnosis of therapeutic misadventure due to rabies vaccine, manifested by arthritis, fever and erythematous induration at injection sites.

I had, indeed, been receiving rabies injections after having taken care of a patient who had succumbed to rabies. I was admitted to the hospital with a mild flare-up of the injection sites after a weekend of heavy drinking. The flare-up disappeared in 24 hours, but I maintained my hospitalization an extra four days by rubbing my thermometer on the pillowcase when the nurse wasn't looking and by holding my breath prior to her taking my pulse.

When I was 31, I was admitted to a hospital following an auto accident that occurred four miles after the last place I remembered getting into my car. The diagnosis:

1. Concussion, brain; 3 June 61 patient involved in an accident, Honolulu, Hawaii.
2. Contusion, multiple, face and right knee.
3. Wound, lacerated, multiple, face and right knee, without artery and nerve involvement.
4. Strain, acute, cervical spine.

Surgical procedures were performed. One of my colleagues removed a blood alcohol slip from my chart. The judge reduced the charge to careless driving.

Three years later, I was admitted to my own hospital for five days after a weekend of heavy drinking. The diagnosis:

synovitis, right hip, etiology undetermined, improved during hospitalization.

At the time my doctors found a uric acid of 15 mg.% and hypertension. They felt I might have a rare syndrome of hyperuricemia-hypertension and wrote to California to draw my father's blood, as this was apparently a syndrome that ran in families. The final diagnosis was changed to: hyperuricemia, etiology undetermined, probable gout, treated, improved.

I was treated with bed rest: the best thing in the world for a hangover. Bed rest, three meals a day, tranquilizers and sleeping pills . . . excellent, inadvertent detox for an alcoholic who's feeling miserable.

My fourth hospital admission, at age 38, came after I passed out at a party on December 24, received CPR from a nurse at the party and was rushed by ambulance to the hospital. The attending physician, a friend of mine, knew that I was simply drunk on Christmas Eve. He sent me home the next morning with the following diagnosis (an attempt to help his colleague):

1. Vaso-vagal syncope. (Fainting)
2. Myositis, left chest. (Chest pain)
3. Flu syndrome.

When I was 40, I was admitted to my own hospital as an emergency. Alcohol was obviously involved by sight and smell. I had attempted suicide by inserting a steak knife into my chest in the area of my heart. I required exploratory surgery, undergoing a laparotomy where the knife track was thought to have gone. It had not, so the doctors had to open my chest and found the knife track into, but not through, the heart muscle. I was repaired and later signed out without any staff attempts at discussion or intervention. The final diagnosis stated factually:

*Diagnosis:* 1. Knife wound, left chest.
*Operations:* 1. Exploratory laparotomy.
2. Exploratory thoractomy.

There you have it . . . five hospitalizations in 13 years. No intervention. Just good intentions. I've spoken with my colleagues in recent years, and none of them suspected that I was actually an alcoholic. I think they probably felt, "There but for the grace of God go I." No one, including myself, put these cases together. No one realized the seriousness of my situation because, as I said, my colleagues were unknowing, unwitting and unwilling . . . so was I.

## Society's Denial

Society's denial begins in the home. My wife had to deny. She was typical, I think, of the American physician's wife. She had what a friend of mine called a "DWH" — a Doctor's Wife Hang-up: a self and societally imposed image of what the successful physician and his family should be. Because of this image and the threat to her security that my drinking represented, she continued to reinforce my own denial. She knew I drank "too much, too fast." But alcoholic? No way!

Physicians are a pillar of the community to patients, merchants, bankers, neighbors, lawyers, judges, cops, etc. It is very difficult for them to see a physician as an "alky." Certainly, law enforcement officials add to our denial because, as they frequently do with women, they'll let the Doc off. They'll drive him home rather than charge a man who is a "pillar of the community" with drunk driving. This happened to me on three occasions.

Another factor that reinforces society's denial is that by the time physicians get into trouble with alcohol, they usually have a long past history of successes — in college, in medical school, with specialty boards and so forth. It seems that if we're successful, we're successful in all aspects of our life. Nothing could be further from the truth.

One thing that I think adds to all three types of denial is that people are not terribly realistic about the doctor's part in his patients' healing process. A surgeon can perform mediocre or marginal surgery and the patient gets well. We do not realize that patients frequently get better in spite of us, as well as because of us. We think we and our colleagues are successful therapists and the prime reason for the patient's recovery. The idea helps to reinforce the denial and to allow the drinking to continue. You cannot possibly be an alcoholic and a competent physician at the same time, right? Wrong!

It's ironic that all through my problem-drinking, my career skyrocketed . . . from my residency in the military as special assistant to the chief of service of the teaching hospital and into private practice. My reputation apparently remained unsoiled.

On the surface everything was going well, but my head, my heart and my home were becoming a shambles. I was on a rapid downward spiral and no one knew it. I was not at any time reported to the chief of staff, chief of nursing, nursing supervisor or hospital administrator, nor did any patient complain to me or my colleagues regarding the possibility that I might have attended them in an intoxicated state.

## Self-Denial

The primary symptom of alcoholism is one's own denial. Occasionally I would have short periods of discomfort about my drinking, but I would resolve them by changing some of my drinking patterns. My ability to quit drinking for varying periods of time allowed me to continue to deny that I was in trouble with alcohol. I was able to easily substitute with pills if I felt that I shouldn't be drinking, but I didn't do this frequently. I used Percodan or codeine as "emergency" substitutes. I was always afraid of the tranquilizers for some reason.

Financial success helped reinforce my denial. My material well-being never suffered from my drinking. My financial well-being was always marginal because of my extravagance. As with many professional people, it's easy to mask the signs of decompensation. I could decide how many patients I'd see each day, if any. I could cancel dates and no one thought anything of it. Everyone accepts the line that "Doctors' lives are not their own. You can't count on them to keep an engagement." It takes a while for the evidence of a problem to filter through the professional mystique. Intervention is delayed.

I never considered myself an alcoholic at all. As I performed certain manipulations, such as hiding bottles in the inner pocket of my sports coat or sneaking extra cocktails or when I was rubbing my thermometer on the pillow or faking a cardiac arrest, I simply felt like a naughty little boy.

I couldn't let myself see it any other way. I wasn't able to handle the reality of my situation, but I had the sneaking suspicion that something was wrong with me. Then one day I couldn't deny it any longer. The fact that I was a phony and couldn't really do anything well hit me like a blow in the chest. I acted out that realization by thrusting a knife into my chest . . . the absolute act of self-loathing and anger.

## Recovery

Following my suicide attempt, my family moved in and spirited me off to another city to begin my recovery. That was only the beginning, though, for my continuing recovery has come through association with many dear friends who are also recovering alcoholics. I began to feel I was alone no longer. This was a new beginning for me, truly!

After my first contact with a recovery organization, which came by means of a letter from their national secretary named Luke, I attended one of their meetings. I have been attending meetings for 15 years since.

At that first meeting I felt connected and that this was where I belonged. But when I returned home after that first meeting, I felt alone again. Then I got a supportive call from a fellow recovering physician named Paul. You can see my whole story is somewhat biblical. I received a letter from Luke and a call from Paul!

In my recovery I began volunteering for various committees for the National Council on Alcoholism, locally and nationally. I also began to volunteer and work on county and state alcohol advisory committees. During this time my recovery from addiction became well known in my hometown and it was through that that I was able to begin establishing information and out-treatment programs and later to be involved in the planning and building of the Betty Ford Center at Eisenhower Hospital.

Once my recovery began, it took two to three years of continuous abstinence to just regain my full spiritual and intellectual powers. Once clarity came to me, perhaps in my second or third year of abstinence, I began to live fully.

But I was still alone. I had a wife and three children and they were alone also. Their husband and father was now suffering from his second primary disease, no longer medicated with alcohol and pills. I was suffering from the same disease affecting all of us. I was recovering nicely from my chemical dependency, but my burning embers of loneliness, yearning and dependency on others continued and flared to an open firestorm as the swallowing disease of co-dependency took over my life.

We each made our own worlds.
We lived under the same roof.
We "acted" like looking-good families act, and we hurt and hurt.
We loved one another, but from afar and in silence.

We didn't know we were still an affected or dysfunctional family . . . or even missing out. We knew something was missing, not necessarily wrong, but just missing, something big . . . but maybe it would get better by itself.

We were pretty much of the opinion that no one else in the world had the same problem, so we didn't even consider going for help. So here were five of us, alone, waiting and probably yearning.

As time went on, I began to understand a lot of the things I didn't know. I call them my "didn't knows" and my "now knows." Just as the program I was in promised that more would be revealed to me, it has been.

Looking at the impact of my disease, I now know what it must have been like for my dad to see a son successfully graduate from medical school and still have such strife in his life and be unable to control his drinking.

I now know what it must have been like to be my daughter, walking up the sidewalk to a party that we had been looking forward to attending and seeing her father receiving mouth-to-mouth resuscitation under the Christmas tree.

I now know how painful it must have been to be my youngest son, who on his birthday sent me a get-well card after my suicide attempt, "Dear Dad, the best possible thing you can give me for my birthday is to be alive."

Or to be my other son, who for eight years thought my suicide attempt was a cover-up for what his mother had done to his father. And then eight years later, realizing the error, able to go to a meeting of those who helped his father. He donated his last 20 dollars he had earned as a beekeeper to demonstrate his gratitude for that organization having saved his father's life. And how great it must have felt, and the relief his mother must have felt when the secret was out, even though it came out eight years late.

I didn't know then but I know now that the family attention I gave was one of control, calling family meetings where I would do the talking, reading my agenda, telling my family members to do this, don't do that, criticizing and laying expectations and my whole self-worth on the family. I required the family to be there for me so that I would be worthwhile. My thoughts were:

"Get with it, family, or just as I suspect, I'm nothing."

"Get well, family, or I'm nothing, just as I thought."

or

"Be a family and a successful family, or I'm nothing, just as I feared."

I heard a recovering alcoholic woman at a large conference talk about how alcoholics are center stage of attention while they are drinking. She said after they stop drinking and put on the red badge of sobriety and wear it on their arm proudly, they are still center stage and the center of attention. All the rest of the family is back there saying, "What about me? What about me?" And one of those family members is also the alcoholic with the red armband on also saying, "I'm sober, but what about me?"

My only identity in those first few. years was being a recovering alcoholic. At least I was worth something, if no more than to be a recovering alcoholic. "I'm Joe, and I'm an alcoholic." And then I began to learn that "I *am* Joe and I have alcoholism." I am an adult child of an alcoholic, raised by one like me and therefore I am also a co-dependent.

But what is co-dependency? What is chemical dependency? Both are primary diseases with remarkably similar symptoms, signs and complications. Both involve the means (behavior or substances) some of us use to satisfy our basic needs, urgings, cravings and fears. Both follow a pattern of "I need it! I'll try it! I *found* it! Brain, don't you forget it!" Then as we find it necessary to increase the frequency, duration, intensity or variety of our use, "I need it!" becomes "It's got me!"

My goal in this book is to help clarify the basics, stages and progression of chemical dependency and co-dependency.

# PART I

# Chemical Dependency

## INTRODUCTION

There is a Public Health model to describe disease epidemics. It works just as well for toxic diseases such as alcoholism and drug abuse. This model of disease states that for an epidemic to occur three requirements must be met:

1. There must be a bacteria, virus or some toxin present. (Toxic Agent)
2. There must be a host who has not had the disease or been vaccinated against it, and is therefore vulnerable to getting the disease. (Susceptible Host)
3. There must be an environment that will allow #1 to gain access to #2. (Permissive Environment)

It can be seen how these three requirements pertain to an epidemic of say, measles or smallpox. The model holds just as well for the disease of chemical dependency. The disease occurs if the three components are present, that is:

1. A toxic agent such as alcohol or other mood-altering chemicals.
2. A susceptible host, actually, a susceptible brain.
3. A permissive environment.

In the United States there's no doubt that it's easy enough for susceptible brains to find mind-altering chemicals. There are probably 15 million alcoholics in this country and more than a million drug addicts, as well as over 25 million individuals who have tried cocaine. There's little doubt that we have an "epidemic."

How can the Public Health model be applied to the disease of chemical dependency to give us a clearer picture of signs, symptoms, complications and stages of the illness?

### Definition Of Terms

By using the Public Health model we are able to define our terms so they can become useful and global. Terms that are global can be used by persons from many different disciplines, who then can communicate with other persons from other disciplines in a meaningful way. A global approach to terminology allows for the logical introduction of new terms into the framework. A model also helps patients and family members understand the disease, the disease process and the outlook based on the stage the individual might be in at any given time.

Diseases are well-defined models of a process of disruption of the normal functioning of an individual. That includes both psychological and physiological systems, according to Dr. Joseph S. Gonnella, M.D. Dr. Gonnella states that diseases are general listings of symptoms and signs that describe physical and emotional abnormalities. Diseases are dynamic, ongoing processes. They leave imprints of frequently preventable, progressive and potentially fatal events. When these events become severe enough, they may be called complications or advanced stages of the disease process.

The *severity* of a disease, as defined by Dr. Gonnella, is the risk of death or temporary or permanent impairment it presents. Severity is actually what is being described when physicians and scientists say a disease is in its early, late or middle stage. Stages are those times in a disease process, which can be defined and clinically detected and also are distinct enough to be caught and communicated. They reflect an increasing severity of a process. Stages are clinically important because they enable us to judge the outlook and the kind of treatment from which the patient will most benefit.

In order to understand chemical dependency as a process of disruption of the normal state of an individual's body or psyche, there must be a foundation on which to base the description of the disease *within* the individual. For this the Public Health model is useful.

## Symptoms And Signs

If symptoms and signs of chemical dependency are just those events resulting from the effects of a *toxic agent* on a *susceptible brain,* then a description of the disease process results. The disease of chemical dependency is extremely personal and has many aspects that go totally unnoticed by the victim and others until serious complications start. Much of this has to do with the permissive environment in which the disease flourishes. There is also a large degree of denial in the individual and loved ones.

Symptoms contain the personal aspects of the disease. They deal with the business conducted between the toxic agent and the susceptible brain or host. Symptoms can be defined as those events in the course of a disease, which the patient feels or experiences and which can be relayed to an outside observer. The pain within the abdomen of a woman with appendicitis would be a symptom. Symptoms of pain, anxiety, apprehension and changes in function are our way of monitoring our internal environment. It is how our body tells us when there is something amiss. These are subjective events.

Signs are observed events or objective events. For example, we would observe the patient with appendicitis showing the "signs" of bending over and perhaps moaning and holding her right side. In addition, she would show "signs" of anxiety and apprehension and demonstrate by her behavior that she is unable to stand up straight. By a physical examination one would observe that she has a tender and firm abdomen.

Our first three chapters outline signs and symptoms, internal thoughts and feelings of individual alcoholics/addicts. The symptoms are the internal thoughts and feelings and external complaints. The signs are the behaviors that are observed.

## Complications

*Complications* in medicine are those events which are usually unexpected, undesirable, frequently life-threatening and almost always preventable. Signs and symptoms usually affect a target organ or organ system but complications can affect the entire body, as well as various aspects of the patient's life, such as social and spiritual. Complications in the case of appendicitis would be the rupture of the appendix, peritonitis, blood poisoning and kidney shut-down. These complications would mean that the disease had progressed well beyond early intervention and surgery. Similar advanced situations occur in chemical dependency.

Most cases of chemical dependency come to the point of being severely complicated before intervention, treatment or even awareness occurs. It's common that the first time alcohol or drugs are mentioned as a problem is when physical, family and occupational complications arise. Actually, 10 to 15 years ago chemical dependency was described as a condition in which "a person uses or drinks to a degree that interferes in one of the major seven areas of life and yet that person continues to drink." In the framework of the Public Health model and in actual cases that definition describes very late and complicated stages.

So the signs and symptoms of a disease are actually the description of that disease. The complications that arise are the problems that accompany the disease when it goes unattended. Obviously earlier detection and treatment are necessary and of great benefit. Most people quickly go for help when they detect one of the possible early warning signs of cancer.

Recognition by others or by oneself of ***"Seven Early Warning Signs of Chemical Dependency"*** will enable individuals to receive help sooner.

1. *Attaches* deeply to alcohol and/or drugs.
2. *Incorporates* alcohol and/or drugs into daily living and thinking.
3. *Denies* that there is anything wrong.

4. *Uses* alcohol and/or drugs as medicine to change feelings and to aid withdrawal.
5. *Tolerates* a large amount of alcohol or drugs.
6. *Fails* to abstain comfortably.
7. *Blackouts.* Has increasing periods of loss of memory.

Much of our difficulty in establishing early warning signs of chemical dependency has been the problem of distinguishing symptoms and signs from complications, the difficulty in separating the actual disease from the problems that follow it. This separation becomes easier when the following two guidelines are used:

1. Signs and symptoms are events in the course of chemical dependency that result from the effects of the toxic agent (i.e., alcohol, drugs), on a susceptible *brain* which acts as host.
2. Complications are events that are an effect of the toxic agent on an individual's *life.*

## Risk Factors

Next we must take a look at risk factors. The fact that chemical dependency has been quite well established as a familial or genetically inherited disease indicates that certain individuals who come from chemically dependent families are at a higher risk. But these are not symptoms, signs or complications. These are *risk factors.*

Risk factors are elements that make a person more susceptible to a particular disease. These factors can be genetic, nutritional, environmental, physical and psychological. Two risk factors for coronary artery disease would be a sedentary lifestyle and a high cholesterol diet. A risk factor for chemical dependency would be having one or more parents or grandparents who were alcoholics.

A great number of studies have tried to determine if there are any nutritional risk factors for chemical dependency. There have been surges of activity in research on the similar metabolic pathways of sugar and alcohol. There have been many social studies on the environmental impact in alcoholism or other chemical dependency. Studies have also been done on the environmental risk for anesthesiologists and dentists constantly exposed to their own anesthetic agents in small amounts daily, after which they would notice a letdown and then self-medicate.

Physical risk factors are those in which constant use of pain or muscle-relaxant medication is necessary. Self-medicating individuals tend to use alcohol because it is cheaper, more easily obtained and has less stigma as an addictive substance than do some of the major painkillers.

An example of a psychological or psychiatric risk factor would be the presence of panic attacks necessitating medication to alleviate the sensations. A high incidence of alcoholism or prescription-drug dependency exists in this group of patients.

## Contributing Factors

*Contributing Factors* are another important element in understanding a disease within an individual. They relate to both the severity and the speed at which the disease consumes the individual. Contributing factors accelerate the disease process. An example would be enabling by family members, co-workers or society in general.

Enabling is well-intended behavior in which persons around a chemically dependent individual hope that by "keeping the waters calm" things will eventually get better. Consequently, people look the other way, make excuses, allow unacceptable behavior and deny that anything is amiss.

Other contributing factors would be working in a high-risk environment, such as a bar, or being in an occupation where one is expected to drink and use. Examples would be jobs in entertainment or certain public relations functions. Highly emotional or traumatic events can also contribute to the acceleration of chemical dependency. Examples are divorce, death or job loss. Some of these items may be the result of the drinking, but they still can be considered as contributing factors to the further development of the disease.

## Precipitating Factors

*Precipitating Factors* are similar to contributing factors. But they usually refer to events that occur suddenly and seem out of the control of the individual. Precipitating factors are those elements which seem to initiate the disease or set off a relapse. An example of a precipitating factor would be the return of a recovering alcoholic to alcohol dependency after extended use of sedative-hypnotic medication.

### *Signs & Symptom Groups*

Lovesick symptoms and signs can be seen in addicts and alcoholics, who are consumed by their emotional attachment to the substance. A second group of symptoms and signs are those where alcohol and drugs are freely used to medicate feelings and withdrawal. The third group of symptoms and signs are the effects of the toxic agent on the person's brain. The person who has become "poisoned" acts as if he has had a stroke. There may be personality changes between times of use. Loss of control and loss of choice about consumption may be present. And there is memory loss.

### *Complication Groups*

The effects of the toxic agent on the patient's life can also be described in three major categories. First, the individual becomes a Loner, even in a crowd. Complications of spiritual bankruptcy or a "Higher Power disconnect" occur. Second, there are those in the Warrior category who are constantly at odds with family, neighbors, fellow workers and authority figures. They become more embroiled in legal complications. Thirdly, we see the young Relic with physical complications of aging and poor functioning that proceed to actual organ damage.

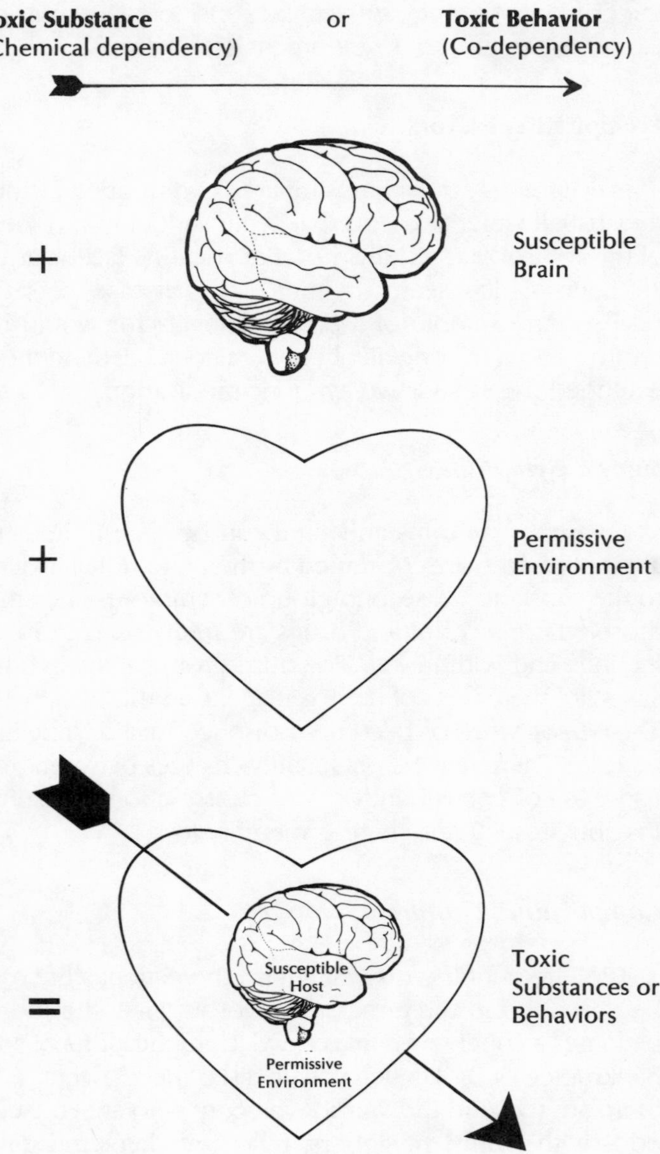


**A Disease Or A Disorder**

# 1

# Romance Symptoms And Signs

## The Deluded Lover

This story is about a love affair . . . a love affair as torrid and as compelling as any love story to come out of Hollywood. It is secret for a time. It goes underground for its survival. This affair, like many others, becomes an illicit one. It seriously affects others.

This love affair is the intriguing story about the attachment of a person to a chemical . . . and of the affinity of that chemical for the person. It is the story of a commitment and an intimate relationship between a person and cocaine, alcohol or any other mind- and mood-altering compound that humans find and decide to take into their bodies.

**"Why won't they stop doing that!?!" "Why can't they see what they are doing to themselves!?!"**

These are two of the most frequently asked questions from desperate family members, frustrated friends, counselors, physicians and out-of-patience employers. And all the while the love affair continues . . . and grows . . . and becomes more complicated and involved. Lives and relationships become increasingly threatened, fractured and then explosively ruptured. The fallout continues long after the sounds of the explosion have died away.

The fallout from such an affair, almost silently and without its presence being known, continues into adulthood for the children, and even into the next generation for the yet unborn. But why, when it is so damaging, does someone start an affair with a chemical? And why does it continue in spite of its painful consequences?

## The Feeling Disease

Chemical dependency has been called a "feeling" disease. No germs or tumors are involved. And like many diseases, even infections, not everybody gets this disease just because they are exposed to addictive drugs. (Drugs are chemicals that have a physiological effect on the body. Alcohol is one such chemical and, therefore, is classed as a drug.)

Cocaine addicts, alcoholics and others who are dependent upon some type of mind- and mood-altering chemical seem to share a common set of reactions and behaviors that are quite perplexing to those around them. Addicts learn that these chemicals can change their feelings and perceptions, especially those associated with emotional pain. They seem to have been searching for relief since birth, and when they come upon certain chemical substances, especially cocaine and alcohol, their body and their brain and even their spiritual self cries out in joy . . . "I found it!" And the love affair begins.

How the heart became the repository, manufacturer and victim of our attempts to develop intimate relationships with others of our own kind is unknown. But there is little doubt that we ascribe a great deal more responsibility to our hearts for our survival and comfort than just pumping blood all day long.

We do it with, "I love you with all my heart" (not just a little part of it, but all of it). We overload it, "You fill my heart with joy" (and still leave room for four or five quarts of blood to be pumped through every minute). We give it a fragile bone-like quality, "My heart is broken," and yet we survive to suffer additional fractures again and again. For some, a fracturing and healing heart lifestyle seems to be normal. We give this organ capabilities unheard of in other organs of our bodies: "My heart aches for you" or "My heart cries for you" or "It is lonely, happy, sad or even empty!" (Imagine a liver crying, aching, lonely, happy, sad or empty.)

Probably all organs can ache, and thank goodness they can, for then we know they need help. The stomach or gut can certainly ache, but also can feel empty or full or tight. We also claim the stomach contains feelings, such as, "I've got a gut feeling about that . . ." We do localize a lot of feeling in our hearts and our stomachs, positive as well as negative ones, such as a joyful heart or a pit in the stomach.

### *Liver*

Long ago the seat of our emotions was thought to be the liver. The liver, one of our largest organs, lies primarily in our right upper abdomen, crossing over to the left upper abdomen and lying like a huge umbrella above our stomach.

As early anatomists began to explore the interior of the human body and to arbitrarily assign various duties to the organs they found, perhaps they looked at the liver, all of its juices and its proximity to where they personally knew emotional pain and anxiety and other emotions lay. They could naturally have deduced, "This must be the place where our personalities, including our emotions, are constructed and influenced."

Perhaps the fact that ancient anatomists ascribed personality and emotional makeup and feelings to the liver was as much the result of its size as it was its location. Personality

(Emotional Reaction) and feelings were important items in those days. Therefore, it was natural to assign all their feelings to the liver. Can you imagine the number-one hit song on their charts, "I Love You With All My Liver" or them sending cutouts of a liver to their sweethearts on February 14th?

If a group of people are asked what is the primary target organ affected by and damaged by alcohol, the answer usually is "the liver." But the truth is that the groups of drugs that alter mind-functioning and mood quality aim at the brain as their primary target organ.

### *Brain*

Our precious brain is the true seat of our emotions, instincts, survival mechanisms, memory, intellect, logic and our total being. The brain is a two- to three-pound intricate and delicate organ that can be easily diverted and short-circuited in its natural functions by external negative influences, such as cocaine, alcohol and other chemicals. What happens when certain brains succumb to these drugs? We do not know all the answers. But we do know a lot of them and are learning more each day.

Researchers are now beginning to understand the manner in which chemicals affect the ability of the brain to handle emotions such as sadness or joy, appetite for food or water, basic survival fight-or-flight reactions and other drives, desires and wants. What we do know is that thoughts, memory, emotions and other very sophisticated functions are based on actual chemical reactions taking place in the brain. Messages are transmitted over several intricate and very fast networks to our entire body. Certain end organs are stimulated to work in concert with one another, and the result can best be described as our reaction.

We are constantly reacting with our environment many hundreds of times per second. We become so used to it that only the major events in our environment catch our complete and undivided attention and become obvious to our mind. Our reaction is then made known to others' minds when we inform them by our words or our actions. Sometimes we lose our choice as to whether or not others are informed of our reaction. It's obvious to them.

Some examples might be our withdrawal from a person from whom we are receiving negative vibrations. They can tell we are withdrawing. Another behavior would be running when we suddenly feel the sensation of fear, such as a sound at night in a dark walkway. A reaction we seldom can control is the dilation of all the blood vessels under our skin that is observed as a blush when we are embarrassed.

Some sort of a bond between a mind- and mood-altering chemical and a person destined to become chemically dependent is established as the dependency begins. It appears that any individual can become tissue or physically addicted to these chemicals if they are exposed to them in large enough doses and for a long enough period of time. Then under the proper circumstances, anyone can display symptoms of severe withdrawal if the drug is suddenly taken away. But the beginning of a chronic long-term dependency that happens to certain individuals and demonstrates a distinct clinical course is more than just tissue dependency.

**Brain Dependency**

The manner in which a primary chemical dependency is established is still not fully known, but it can be described. It is a *brain* dependency that does not easily go away even when the drug is not being used.

When the "I found it!" fever hits the brain of a susceptible person, it results in behavior that is most easily understood when compared to and described as *A Love Affair*. A more descriptive exclamation of the meeting between a mind- or mood-altering chemical and a chemically dependent person's brain might be . . . "I found *her*!" or "I found *him*!"

The whole process resembles an exciting romance, at least at first, and contains all the ingredients of a classic love story. There is the courtship, there is the fully blossoming infatuation and love. There is commitment. But there is no living happily ever after. You see, it doesn't last. Like many lopsided, controlled and controlling, dependent relationships, it struggles and strangles. It even begins to influence and damage others outside the chemical relationship. It goes underground and becomes an illicit affair.

The behavior, perceptions and struggles of a person actually consumed by an illicit affair with another person are mirrored by the addicted person who is fighting for the right to continue a relationship with (and the use of) their chosen chemical (drug).

If we could hear such an individual talking in his or her head to their drug of choice, we might understand better. It probably would sound very much like infatuated people speaking to their first loves or first beloved and later their paramours or mistresses as the relationships proceed through the courtship to the full-blown affair.

## Courtship Of A Chemical

Let's imagine a young man, for example, talking for the first time to his drugs of choice, in this instance alcohol and cocaine. We will progress with him through his teen years into his 20s and 30s and 40s. Although it takes less time than that for actual trouble to start, the usual case isn't intervened upon until a good number of years have passed and difficulties have been tolerated much too long. Today the course of the disease is much clearer and carries less stigma, so intervention is occurring earlier and earlier.

What follows is a monologue from that young man and the words and thoughts that being in love with drugs might evoke. Listen.

> "Hi! . . . I've always wanted to meet you . . . and now I have . . . wow! We are actually going to get together! . . . I've seen your attractive photographs on billboards and in magazines . . . and I know you have played some really important roles in the movies and on television . . . and I know that you hang around with some really important people and some really

rich and fun-loving people. And now we have met and we are going to get together. I can hardly wait. I've been talking to the guys about what you are like and how we might get together. I am excited! I know you have seen me hanging around with the guys that are going out with you. I wanted to see how they do it. I want to be sure I get it right . . . right? . . . right on!

"I'm not so young that I don't know that we could get into trouble . . . ! My mom and dad fought a lot and I thought it was over his job or money. I didn't know he was going with you. I didn't know he put you on a pedestal far above everyone else, including me. I guess I can see why he might do that, knowing about you like I do. But it still hurts and Mom will probably never get over the fact that we were number two on Dad's Hit Parade. Me? I'll handle it a lot differently and I'll keep us from ever having trouble like you and Dad, and you and some of my friends did. You can be sure of that! And we will just have a couple of short test dates before we go whole hog . . . okay? I don't really know if I want to get serious with you."

(After the first episode of drinking and using.)

"Wow . . . Ooooooeeeeeeee! . . . You . . . are . . . something! Did you see how they noticed us? . . . I never knew I could dance so well . . . We were the hit of the party! . . . And nobody gave us a hard time. The guys thought I was great! . . . I'll never be a wallflower again . . . How about that? . . . I'll never be a wallflower again . . . Ever! . . . From now on it is you and me, baby! I'll say where and when and how much and you just be with me, okay? What a godsend you are!"

Curiosity, using at social events, starting with others' supply, learning how to use, experimenting, then buying one's own supply, knowing that you have "found it," are events that occur early in the addict's life, perhaps earlier than junior high and certainly high school. Many people become socially more comfortable and more assertive with the use of drugs, especially alcohol, which has been called a "social lubricant." Sexual interest, sexual assertiveness and even perhaps sexual performance are enhanced and increased when these drugs are used. As this begins, it looks like the usual courtship. The affair includes testing, experimenting, being careful and leery, and at the same time excited and anticipating each next use.

## Uninformed Denial

There is a bit of denial that goes with this in the face of information the public is receiving regarding the use of drugs and the excess inappropriate use of alcohol. There is an uninformed denial that comes from not recognizing that individuals can be very susceptible to becoming addicted. There is the uninformed denial from not knowing that if chemical dependency exists in one's parents or even grandparents, the opportunities and perhaps even genetic programming are present to set one at a greater risk than one's peers.

The pressure from peers is too great and over-rides the scare information. Movies on venereal disease did not seem to cut the rate of gonorrhea or syphilis seen in the Armed Forces in the past. The attraction of mind- and mood-altering drugs is just as great. The entrapment and seduction of cocaine is greater.

## Prevention

Perhaps future prevention efforts will successfully diminish the value that our society seems to place on chemical serenity, chemical joy and chemical use. Prevention efforts need to provide basic anatomical and physiological information to our youth, but life values and self-worth need to be modeled and taught. We need not waste our time with teaching them responsible use or responsible drinking, as has been tried in the past, or even responsible decision-making.

The best preventive techniques of the future will be the same as we teach in other areas of our children's lives. That is, "You are valuable. Risks must be taken in life. Responsible risk-taking is difficult, you need not take all the risks that are offered, especially using drugs and alcohol. If you do take any risk, be careful because you are valuable."

Their best basis of whether to use or not use and our best method of teaching responsible risk-taking is society's and our own individual role-modeling — what we show them by our own lifestyles, values and behaviors.

The courtship, with its experimentation and learning to use, occurs in the junior high and teenage years (sadly, sometimes earlier). Soon bonds are formed that can only be described as a full-blown romance. It may go on for 10 or 20 years or perhaps blow up within a few years. Regardless, the description of a romance continues to hold. Listen.

"Hi again . . . I've been thinking about you all day. I have decided how we will be able to get together every night. But we can't stay long, otherwise we will get into trouble. I may need to cut my last class or leave work early, but I think I can work it out . . . You know it would be great if I could see you at noon once in a while. I probably shouldn't and we would have to be careful . . . Hey, I gotta tell you, last night was really a little embarrassing. I don't know what happened. We got into some trouble . . . But it was kinda fun, wasn't it? . . . I had a hard time explaining it.

"You know, I'm gonna just quit going to those functions if you are not there. I know you don't go to church or some of the school programs and other functions. I'm just gonna knock those off. And I know I have quite a few friends that don't care to have you around so I'll give them up 'cause there is nothing I want to do without you.

"You know, it is interesting, I hardly start to part with you when I'm wondering when we can get together again. I just think it's great to be high with you . . . There are some times, especially if I have exams or a big presentation the next day that I am going to have to stay away from you. I hope you understand. I hope I can stand it, for that matter . . . But even if we don't get together on some weekdays, I'll always see you on weekends . . . and of course, if it's a holiday on a weekday . . . or if it is my birthday . . . or if it is anyone's birthday . . . we will get together . . . mmmm, yes.

"You know, I must say I never thought life would be so full, that I would look forward to each day with such anticipation as I do, or that I would meet such wonderful people or have such fun or be as sexy and I must say, even as suave as I am. I hate it when I am weak or scared or depressed but you take care of all that for me. Even when it comes back, I can always count on you . . . I can always predict the effect you are going to have on me . . . There is nothing wrong with our relationship and nothing will ever happen to it!"

The full-blown romance expands the preoccupation. It results in placing a high value on the love object and integrating it into all aspects of the lifestyle of the smitten one. Not unexpected occurrences, considering the depths that chemical love can reach in a person.

Assuring that there will be a supporting and an understanding environment is absolutely essential for the addict. To use drugs, such as cocaine and alcohol, in the manner that an addict has to use them requires some drastic measures. A great deal of time, energy and forethought are required to keep this romance running. Disassociating oneself from friends, isolating, ignoring the needs and wants of others, realizing that embarrassment might occur on occasion isn't important. Secretly, it might even be fun.

**Deluded Denial**

Being able to anticipate and look forward with joy and excitement to the next use is all part of the deluded denial that anything is wrong or harmful. Because these chemicals work, and because they work so well, there is no doubt in the user's mind that they will always work and always work well. This is true even when they have seen others who have been "jilted and hurt" by their chemicals. The deluded lover in the height of the romance has no insight. There exists instead the "It-won't-happen-to-me" belief, a strong and powerful belief indeed.

This denial might be due to the chemicals themselves that reach into the lover's brain with the message that "everything is all right." These drugs do this by short-circuiting insight and logic. Who could expect someone embroiled in such a romance to give up their lover who offers so much? It is interesting that at this stage few people in a chemically dependent person's life suspect that there is a love affair with a chemical. Therefore, no efforts are considered to interrupt the process. The disease runs on and gets worse.

## Tolerance

What causes a romance such as this to become an illicit affair? Why doesn't it just continue as sort of a happy-go-lucky relationship in which there is never any serious trouble? The answer is *tolerance.*

When food is taken into our body, it is set upon by many, many different kinds of digestive enzymes. These enzymes break down the food so that our body may absorb them, transport them and use them in certain areas and then excrete them in another form. When the body meets an external chemical, it has enzymes to help it metabolize that chemical. Its usual reaction is to increase the number of enzymes specific for that chemical, just in case more of the chemical comes along. When more chemical comes along, it can be efficiently broken down, transported and excreted. The body then increases the number and amount of enzyme even more as a form of readiness for the next onslaught.

When someone first begins drinking, one or two drinks provide a definite effect. When a person first uses cocaine they frequently, depending upon their state and their expectations, have a high reaction. Certainly after the first few uses, they will notice an extreme exhilarating euphoric state. This is short-lived, however, with both alcohol and cocaine as the body prepares for the next using experience by manufacturing additional enzymes.

## Repeat And Increase

The body builds and builds and builds its enzyme reserve. In addition, nerve connections and the brain become refractory or resistant to the original amounts of alcohol or other drug that had definite effects. To regain those same effects, then, requires larger and more frequent amounts of the drug or alcohol. The person who is using alcohol and drugs finds that to obtain the same original effect, they need to frequently *repeat* their drug again and again and again. They must significantly *increase* the dose again and again and again. The beginner has low tolerance. The addict has high tolerance.

The users who stick with it and persevere in their use will develop a high tolerance and will show less effects. They become the best drinker at the corner bar. It takes more to saturate the cells of their body, and they overcome this with higher and higher doses. So now they have high tolerance.

Over the years this high tolerance begins to diminish. By the time someone is in their late stages, especially of alcoholism or sleeping-pill addiction, we find that they are very *intolerant* even of small doses. Again this is late in the course of the disease and will be mentioned later.

As tolerance develops, the person who noticed joy, exhilaration, relief or relaxation from their first doses of a drug now finds that they must increase the dose of the drug for the same effect. This requirement to increase the dose of the drug does not just happen once, but is a steady curve upward where a greater and greater dose is required. It is at this point that the disease actually becomes a toxicology (poisoning) problem. Too much of any chemical, such as aspirin or digitalis or even water, can cause our bodies to be poisoned. In essence, that is what occurs in chemical dependency as the tolerance increases. More will be said about this as we come to the chapter on the overdoser. Needless to say, marked changes begin to occur.

The chemically dependent person is frequently the first to notice the change in needs, both in frequency and amounts. Almost subconsciously, fear of discovery or loss of use changes behavior from that of an open, somewhat carefree but obviously deluded and dependent lover in a steady romance to that of a participant in an energetic, 24-hour campaign against detection or loss. Listen.

> "Hi! . . . I don't know what's happening but I had a hard time explaining us the other night . . . I even had a harder time getting to you tonight . . . I want to be with you so much more

than I can . . . but there are some times that I just have to see you briefly and I hate it! . . . I've even had to lie about whether we were together or not . . . I've changed a lot of things so that we can be together more often and longer . . . I've had to cover up a lot . . . I've had the feeling that they might try to slow us down or take you away from me entirely . . . It gets harder to get to you and to be with you and enjoy you and to eliminate any evidence that we have been together. I've even thought they might try to take you away from me . . . God! I couldn't stand that . . . I thought perhaps we should meet out of town frequently so that we can be together as we want. They don't seem to understand . . . I can handle this myself, there is really nothing wrong . . . Nothing . . ."

(After more time and more using and drinking.)

"Damn . . . Why won't they leave us alone?! . . . I have to tell you something . . . We are not having as much fun as before . . . What's the matter with you? . . . Why isn't it like it used to be? . . . I don't understand but I don't want to change. I try not to think of you but I am obsessed with you and I can't get you out of my mind . . . I tell you I love you but I hate you . . . I can't keep on living this way and I can't live without you . . . Hey people! . . . Back off . . . leave us alone! . . . I can handle this! . . . Go away! . . . Don't they know I need you? . . . They don't understand . . . I'll have to hide you! . . ."

And as the relationship between the person and the chemical becomes more bizarre and requires more protection, the relationship becomes more painful and a vicious circle is closed. The major problems within this circle are supply problems — availability of a drug, availability of the time to use it, availability of escapes and explanations, the destruction of evidence of any use, sneaking drinks, using alone or drinking alone, obsession with certain types of drugs or certain types of alcohol or certain brands or certain grades of drugs, and mostly being obsessed with when the next use will be.

### Desperate Denial

The former "preoccupation" with getting high or drinking or mellowing out has now become an obsession. Long episodes of unnatural use on trips or by staying up all night, requiring difficult explanations and lies and alibis, are all present in the person having an affair with a chemical. They reach the stage of not just uninformed and deluded denial, but now they are at the point of desperate denial. And no one is more perplexed or in more pain than the individual. They now find themselves enmeshed in a relationship that has no benefits and, in fact, has become a love/hate affair.

There are more aspects to this relationship than just a scrambled and scrambling romance. We begin to see behaviors and effects on a person's brain resulting from self-medication and overdosing. Almost all illegal drug addicts, alcoholics and prescription-pill addicts will admit that early on they learned how these compounds could give them relief . . . That not only do they serve as a love potion but they are a medicine that brings greater and quicker and more complete relief than anything they had encountered in their life before.

They very soon become their own physician and their own pharmacist as they begin to use these drugs as a prescription. All of these compounds, including alcohol, are chemicals used by addicts and alcoholics as a medicine. Americans self-medicate. We are coerced to comfortably accept chemicals in our lives by the beverage, pharmaceutical and advertising industries. We are taught that there is a "pill for every ill." We learn that something outside of ourselves can help with that certain something that is uncomfortable within ourselves. To some degree, all of us have been self-medicators. Early on alcohol and drugs become the most powerful medicine in the world to the Self-Medicator.

**Chemical Dependency Symptoms And Signs**

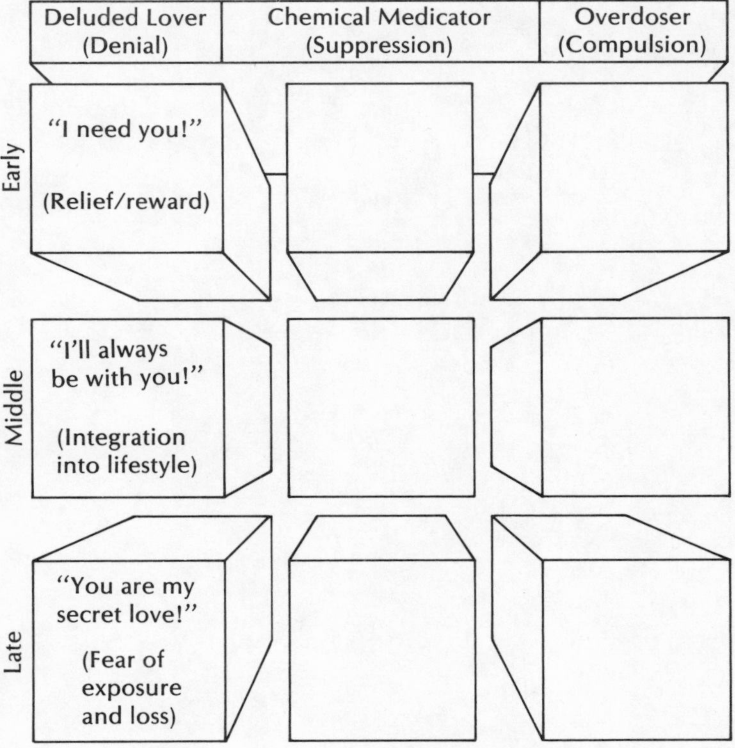


This is a description of the ***PRIMARY*** disease of chemical dependency, showing the major symptom groups that result from the disease affecting the person's ***BRAIN.***

2

# Medicating Symptoms And Signs

## The Medicator

By the time Deluded Lovers are thoroughly involved in an Illicit Affair, they have learned that they qualify better than anyone else as their own physician and pharmacist, their own Self-Medicator. Medicating feelings is a way and a means of not having to put up with discomfort, and it works fast. Alcoholics and other addicts have low pain thresholds and insist on instant gratification.

Emotional anesthesia is available. "Emotional anesthesia" is a term used by Dr. E. M. Jellinek, one of the pioneer physicians to begin describing the events in the course of this disease. He recognized self-medicating, although he didn't exactly call it that. An early clue that a person has become a Self-Medicator is that . . . the chemical has ceased to exist as a beverage or a recreational drink or even a recreational drug. It is *medicine!*

This chemical is now used to perform a change in the human body and, therefore, can be classed as a drug. Cocaine is a chemical used by cocaine addicts as a drug or medication. Alcohol is a chemical used by alcoholics as a drug or medication. Even prescribed medication from a physician can be taken abusively in doses and frequency decided by the self-appointed pharmacist. The Self-Medicator, not the physician, decides how much, how often and how many kinds of medication will be taken.

People who have succumbed to an addiction of this type use alcohol and other drugs in many different situations. On occasion they may use to feel good when they feel bad. On other occasions they use just to change "normal." They may use to feel better when they are feeling good. On other occasions they may use when they are totally distraught to feel less so. In any event, they decide what they will use and when they will use it. They attempt, but soon lose the ability, to decide how much they will use. They do indeed become their own physician and their own pharmacist. Sadly, the "physician" and the "pharmacist" are hooked.

## Prescription-Writing

In a way, they write self-authored prescriptions. They are sure no one can know more intimately than they just what are their daily and hourly needs. It's surprising how long it takes for the Self-Medicator's practices to become apparent to others. But even as the using and abusing practices begin to look more and more bizarre to the observer, they become more and more "logical" for the addict.

Drugs do work, at least initially. They work for the purposes of relief from feelings of depression or inadequacy, physical pain, fatigue or insomnia. Even the belief that one is abnormal or at least different from everyone else can be medicated away for a time. There is a prescription even for this.

Increasing the dose of any mind- and mood-altering chemical is tricky at best. New symptoms begin to appear that have to do with obtaining and maintaining the proper dose level of the drugs in the body. Certain actions and behaviors that the addict/alcoholic goes through seem quite normal, acceptable and justified to them. Should others around them become aware of their symptoms of self-medicating, they would consider that type of thinking and behavior as quite bizarre. The point is, the "physician" in a person decides to increase the amounts and frequency and the "pharmacist" in a person then must fill the prescription and give directions so that high blood levels of the agent can be obtained rapidly and maintained regularly. These doses might be ones that would normally have knocked the person off their feet in their early period of using. But now because of tolerance, the addict/alcoholic can easily withstand higher doses. How can such levels be reached? Let's use alcohol as an example. (The same holds for any of the other sedative-hypnotic drugs such as certain sleeping pills and tranquilizers.)

**Fast Dosing**

One of the familiar dosing symptoms that alcoholics talk about is gulping. Gulping is fast dosing. Non-alcoholics usually sip or drink their drinks. Alcoholics gulp. They need to gulp and not be noticed. They also need extra strong drinks and, of course, extra drinks. "Doubles" were made for Self-Medicators.

What are some ways the alcoholic can reach the needed dosage without being noticed? Mixing drinks for other individuals while at the same time, *each time*, mixing a drink for oneself is one way. Offering to be the bartender is a dosing symptom when done for the purpose of mixing more and stronger drinks for oneself. And, of course, the "all-American dressing drinks" — having drinks while getting dressed to go out to drink — is a classic way to obtain satisfactory blood levels through the evening without being noticed. Continued use after others stop drinking and using after returning home or after everyone has retired are dosage problems.

Similar symptoms of dosing hold true for other sedative-hypnotic drugs, and similar techniques to alleviate are used.

Cocaine or heroin addicts use methods of inserting their drug into their brain that provides a faster and greater effect. By mainlining, or injecting the drug directly into a vein, and sniffing through the nasal mucous, drugs are absorbed much faster and go directly into the brain. By smoking the drug, it is inhaled into the lungs and sent directly into the blood stream and to the brain.

The person embroiled in an Illicit Affair has availability problems such as, "How can I get at it? How can I use it? How can I get rid of the evidence?" The person who has become a Self-Medicator has dosing problems. "How can I get to it sooner? How can I get it in fast? How can I get enough and keep getting enough without anyone noticing?" This kind of behavior is not an obvious sign of a problem to the individual and perhaps not even to those very, very close to the addict. Historically, those people closest to the addict are frequently the last to notice. And the alcoholic/addict considers the behavior normal.

## Urgency Symptoms

Another aspect of self-medicating, distinct from being preoccupied all day with the drug of choice and different from mainlining or snorting or gulping, is the symptom of *urgency*. Between the preoccupation and the actual act of using, there is a period of time when addicts, especially cocaine addicts, feel an exciting and desperate sense of urgency to get at their drug of choice. This results in behaviors that would not be recognized as connected to drug use. Actually driving a car fast to get to the place of use or supply, changing business appointments, cancelling hospital rounds, going to work early in order to get off early . . . all can result from urgency symptoms. These behaviors are a part of integrating the drug into one's lifestyle.

Urgency symptoms are part of a "hunger drive" that results in irrational drug-seeking behavior or overtly destructive behavior. When behavior becomes abnormal or aberrant, the alcoholic/addict needs to justify this abnormal behavior or keep it below the conscious level. Grand rationalizations for changing schedules or cancelling important events or appointments are used. Any maneuver or idea that an alcoholic or an addict can use to move closer to the time of use is conceived of and is used. Delegating responsibilities when it is not indicated or even appropriate or safe is an example. Incomplete work, procrastinating and putting off duties and work in order to get to using and drinking is another. Shortcutting, being short with others and taking the short way home, are common means of lessening the duration of *urgency.*

This can be carried to the extreme of avoiding traffic on the way home, avoiding certain duties on the way home or perhaps not even leaving home. By staying at home, feigning illness or justifying working at home, use can begin at an earlier and earlier time. Again this may appear on the surface as normal unrelated behavior. If those close to and affected by the alcoholic/addict knew that the basic driving force behind what they were observing was chemical, they would indeed consider this bizarre. So would the alcoholic/addict, if there was any insight into the relationship with the chemical. But even when they do know, they aren't talking about it, especially to themselves. Listen.

> "Hi! . . . Oh! . . . I really scooted over here today to see you. I could hardly wait to get here. Oh, whew, what a relief. We are finally back together again. It was only a day ago but it seemed like forever since I left you. I know we can't be together continuously. My God, people might think I had a problem with you or something, but I do hate to leave you and I always enjoy the first part of our meeting. The first part of when we get together is almost like we have never met before. In fact, it is almost more exciting thinking about getting together with you than it is being with you. But it is obviously more relaxing once we are together. I know I can count on you.
>
> "No matter how bad it is going out there, if I can just remember that I have you, I can handle it a lot better. It is sort of tough out there at times, you know, and many days it never goes like I really want it to or think it should, but you seem to make it all not matter and that's what I want. I want to not care. I had

a friend once who said when he dated you, it was like pushing his 'I don't care' button and the world was sweet and easy and quiet most of the time. I like that about you. You are so versatile. You can pep me up and help me have more fun and make me pretty gutsy. Other times you just help me mellow out and be. You help me enjoy poetry and drama and music better than I ever could without you. You make me realize that I am probably more sensitive than any other human being in the world. There is no other way that anyone could understand how I feel and how you make me feel. You are like a good medicine to me . . ."

**Withdrawal**

Tolerance increases to such high levels that there are effects following the cessation of use. Once a person stops using and the drug wears off, some effects begin to occur that are commonly called a hangover. Withdrawal is not necessarily full of convulsions and hallucinations. Withdrawal effects may be nothing more than an internal sense of discomfort, a slight tremor, a headache, lethargy (no energy) and malaise (just feeling badly). These are withdrawal symptoms caused by prolonged or excessive use of a drug.

The self-medicating, self-appointed physicians soon learn that a little bit of the "hair of the dog that bit them" will suffice for these minor symptoms of withdrawal. They then begin to use the same drug on which they overdosed the night before to alleviate these symptoms the next day. Frequently, the use of alcohol to medicate the withdrawal symptoms from alcohol is quite justified in certain social settings, such as a Saturday morning golf tournament or a Sunday morning brunch, and the Bloody Marys flow forth. Other times the minor symptoms of withdrawal are simply "the flu again," usually occurring on a Monday morning, the justification for many a day lost from work.

As more frequent and more severe episodes of intoxication from drugs occur, more frequent detoxification from those drugs is required by the self-medicating, self-appointed physician. And so daily use starts. The withdrawal from the night before may not appear until mid-afternoon or late afternoon, when evening use "rejuvenates" the person who is in withdrawal from the dosages received the day before. Therefore, daily use becomes necessary. Regular and systematic intoxication requires regular and systematic detoxification. Early morning use begins. In some cases continuous use begins.

### Continuous Usage

Drinking or using all day and into the night does not mean drunkenness or getting loaded each time. This type of use is to maintain a comfortable blood level and keep life tolerable, even for a short period of time. Drinking moderate amounts throughout the day can prevent uncomfortable withdrawal. Some individuals appear perfectly fine and not intoxicated at all for days on end as they drink for days on end. In truth, they are an alcoholic in balanced intoxication/withdrawal.

The self-appointed pharmacist and physician may, however, have hallucinations, prolonged headaches and periods of amnesia. They keep quiet. They learn to medicate these symptoms, perhaps thinking that they are the result of an impending stroke or a brain tumor. The drugs remove these symptoms but not the fear — fear that something very serious is wrong. Indeed, something is very seriously wrong, but it's not a brain tumor. It's something equally fatal, but far more treatable than most brain tumors . . . it is advancing chemical dependency.

Another discovery is used by our physician/pharmacist. So this condition, along with feelings or fatigue or insomnia or emotional or physical pain, can be medicated. Listen.

> "Hi . . . I don't feel too well . . . I have been noticing more and more that I frequently have a headache, especially when I get up in the morning. Sometimes I don't think I can even move my body from the bed to the bathroom. Other times I have such a pounding in my ears and in the back of my neck that I wonder if something isn't growing in my head. I figure I must not have eaten well, or maybe I have diabetes or something, but I shake so badly, at first especially. And I know I may have something

happening in my stomach or in my intestines because I keep gagging and retching, especially in the morning when I brush my teeth. I can hardly touch my toothbrush to my mouth without starting this horrible retching and gagging. I am wondering about my heart, too, because, even as a former athlete, I can hardly exert myself without feeling it racing away. On occasion I have taken my pulse and I have noticed it skipping and skipping. I'm only going to tell you and no one else, I'm scared. When I can get to you, you show me that magic that you have shown me from the beginning, then I feel better. I'll just watch it and keep you with me to make me comfortable. Who knows, if something's wrong with me, it may be too late already, so what does it matter? The docs never seem to know what is wrong with me. Of course, I won't tell them that I worry about my heart or my possible brain tumor. They don't have to know about you, either, you're my godsend. If they just hand me some sort of prescription, I'll be fine. Good Lord! It just struck me, I wonder if since we have been together more and more and more, that maybe the trouble is partly from you. No! It can't be! The docs would have figured that out from the tests or they would have asked about you. They have never said a word. No, actually you help, you didn't cause this!"

And the distorted belief that you didn't cause it, you actually help it, continues and enlarges. A lack of insight? Possibly. Deluded denial? Probably. Sprinkled in with the earlier uninformed denial and upcoming desperate denial. Also there is probably a direct toxic effect on the function of the brain that disallows the formation of any logical relationship between the beginning problems and the person's use, at least at this stage. And the possibility that such a relationship is a disease is the least likely concept to be formulated in a chemically dependent brain.

The hurry, scurry and "busyness" of the addict/alcoholic continues. "How can I get to my chemical quickly enough? Often enough? And for long enough?" are the 24-hour preoccupations of the alcoholic/addict. Elaborate forethought, preparation and execution of certain methods to assure not only the access but also sufficient quantities becomes more and more the norm. Listen.

"Hi . . . You might not believe this, but for the last month or so, you have been popping into my head at 11:00 in the morning. I have to go on about my business, of course, but I've found myself thinking about how soon I can get to you and how long we'll be together. And I've started learning to do a few things that I think are pretty tricky and allow us to be together like I really want to be. I've learned some shortcuts to get to you. Even with those, it is none too soon, which is why I need to meet you on the way home. That's why I need to be able to know that you will always be there if I can find an extra hour or extend a lunch time or that you will be ready at a moment's notice. They don't even notice when I leave the room. I take you with me. I have you hidden. I know certain places, even in my own home, where you are and there is even the excitement of finding you and keeping you hidden. Most importantly, there is the relief of finding you and being with you. As I told you, I can stand most anything if you are with me. I know it is perhaps kind of silly, but I really like being with you before I ever leave to go out with you all evening. Anything to extend the time we can be together. I'd say you are not just a part of me, you are me, and I you. You are the best medicine, the best everything, I have ever found! . . ."

## Chemical Dependency Symptoms And Signs

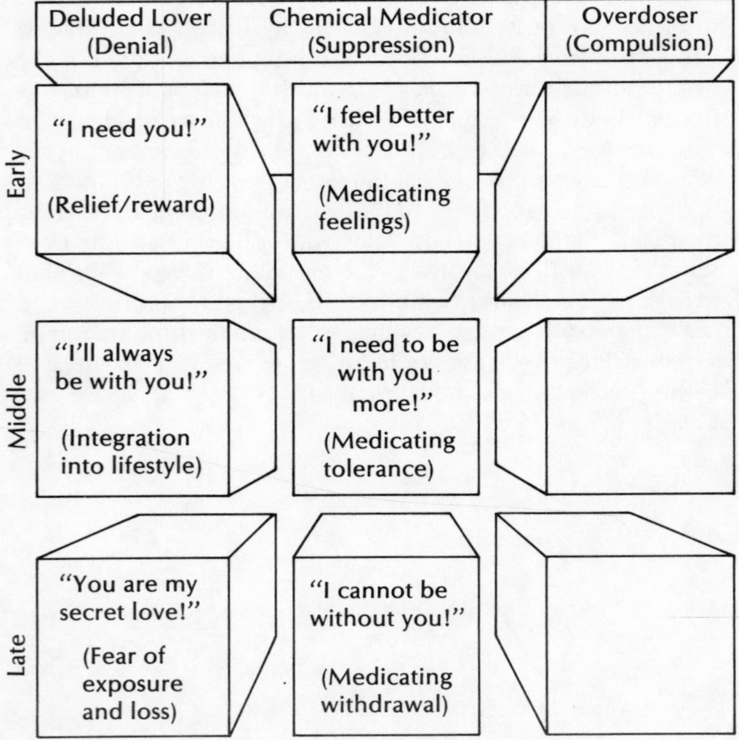


This is a description of the ***PRIMARY*** disease of chemical dependency, showing the major symptom groups that result from the disease affecting the person's ***BRAIN.***

3

# Toxic Symptoms And Signs

## The Overdoser

During the courtship and the romance with alcohol or drugs and during the Illicit Affair, tolerance develops. Tolerance means that the dose which worked initially no longer works, and it needs to be increased. Persons who are addicted to alcohol or drugs and use them constantly learn this almost subconsciously. Almost without noticing they start increasing their doses. They soon become tolerant . . . "the biggest drinker in the office" or "the best drinker at the corner bar." They "can really hold their liquor." They are known as the person who needs greater amounts of cocaine or grass or any other drug being used in a group setting. These are the folks who need more, who have increased their tolerance.

For a person to obtain a desired sensation, they must take into their bodies a set amount of any mind- and mood-altering chemical. Later in the course of their use, they find that they are using twice as much to obtain the same effect. And later on when the tolerance is quite high, they can drink or use great amounts with little effect. By the time they reach the stage of high tolerance, they cannot stop their frenetic search for that original benefit they received when they first "fell in love" with their chemical.

As we saw in Chapter 2 on the Self-Medicator, the euphoria, self-assurance, aggressiveness, joy, exhilaration, energy, confidence and relief that individuals first received from their lover chemical no longer comes about, even when greater and greater amounts are used. So now our self-appointed physician/pharmacist must decide what to do so those benefits can be regained and maintained. The result is overdosing, getting drunk or high again and again.

## Intoxicants

Alcoholism, Morphinism, Cocainism, Heavy Metal Poisoning, Argyria (Silver Poisoning) and Plumbism (Lead Poisoning) are all listed as "Intoxicants" in DeCosta's 740-page *Handbook of Medical Treatment,* Volume 1, (F. A. Davis and Company, *1919*). In fact, the author of the chapter on Intoxicants, Henry K. Mohler, M.D., Medical Director of the Jefferson Hospital in Philadelphia in those years, stated the following: "Poisoning by lead, or plumbism is by far, *next to alcohol,* the most important intoxication from a clinical standpoint." Painters were among the major susceptible groups at risk for lead poisoning. Public health measures have all but irradicated plumbism. Not so with alcoholism.

In 1919 the practicing physician had to depend on a font of knowledge and an organized way of thinking and categorizing diseases. Lab tests and X-rays were few. CAT scans, ultra-sound, angiography and EKG's were nonexistent. The minimum attributes for an astute diagnostician were keen eyes, ears, nose and touch. These, together with an efficient and incisive history-taking ability and an ability to observe and examine the patient, resulted in the answer, the diagnosis. And the answer in those days was that alcoholism is an *intoxication.*

We all know that. But what they meant, and what many of us don't consider, is that drunken or loaded is *poisoned.* A drunk or loaded person in an emergency room is a toxicological (poisoning) problem. We need to keep reminding ourselves of that. Then we can understand and explain to chemically dependent patients, their families, student nurses, medical students or psychology students what's actually happening.

## Chronic Overdosing

The third major group of symptoms that result from increasing tolerance, and therefore increasing the requirement for high toxic amounts of chemicals, can be grouped under the heading of *The Chronic Overdoser.*

Too much of even a good medication can become a bad thing. This is especially true in the delicately balanced living human body. Emergency rooms are prepared for poisoning cases.

The definition of poisoning is:

> "Any agent used which, introduced into an organism, may chemically produce an injurious or deadly effect."

Agents which are extremely beneficial to human beings and agents which are not necessarily beneficial for human beings can be the cause of poisoning. For instance, most people don't realize that traces of strychnine are present in most of our milk supply and can be extracted from anyone's body at any given time. The dose level is so low that there is no clinical, observable or even important effect from trace amounts. However, a level that becomes life-threatening to the individual can be obtained with just a bit more than traces of this particular drug.

Other substances that are seen in emergency room poisonings are digitalis, aspirin, tranquilizers and sleeping pills. Overdoses of these substances can cause death, especially when mixed with alcohol. Even water intoxication can occur if excessive amounts are taken into the body, especially over short periods of time. The most common toxicologic or overdosing problem that emergency rooms see is that of alcohol overdose. The second most common are other mind-altering drug overdoses.

Various overdosing agents affect people quite differently and depend upon the amount, the size of the person, the route used and the speed with which the substance was ingested or taken into the body. A Valium or sleeping pill overdose in the emergency room is considered a suicide attempt until proven otherwise. A digitalis overdose is treated as a medication "misadventure." Aspirin overdose in a child is looked upon as an accident. In the early 1900s, lead overdose in a painter was looked upon as an occupational hazard.

Emergency rooms have posters indicating "Poison Centers" around the country where specialized information can be obtained regarding whatever substance was taken into the body in excessive doses. When a patient is brought in, emergency room physicians and nurses spring into action. The stomach may be irrigated and pumped, intravenous medication and fluids are started, the kidney dialysis team may be put on alert, as perhaps will be the intensive care ward and the medical floors. Special consultation is obtained.

Alcohol overdose, however, is frequently looked upon as stupid, willful and simple drunkenness. When an alcoholic or a cocaine addict hits the emergency room — moving, breathing and complaining — there is often a sigh of frustration. "Here is another one that is going to be hard to handle." "Why do they do this to themselves?"

Many intoxications are not as life-threatening as one might think, unless the doses are extremely high. This is true for alcohol as well as some other drugs. But where is the "toxicologist" who would routinely be called in a case of a different type of overdose? Where is the chemical dependency counselor or addictionologist physician who still is not commonly called to the emergency room for cases of "simple" drunkenness or being loaded?

Perhaps this particular overdose and ingestion is not life-threatening, but what about the next time? And the next? And whose life and how many lives are threatened when the next episode of overdose occurs? Only the addict's life? No. Unlike a lot of other suicidal and poisoning cases, this particular patient may well take several with him when he or she finally does go. The most common way for that to happen, of course, is through a fatal auto accident caused by a drunk driver.

## What Does Intoxication Do?

Let's examine for a moment just how the poisoning problem of an intoxicated person comes about. Just what does "intoxication" involve? Alcohol or other drug intoxications are similar to a temporary "stroking out" of the brain, where there is either a hemorrhage or a closing-off of the blood supply to certain parts of the brain. A stroke may leave instant residual damage, but the analogy holds. The first signs of a stroke are generalized, with the entire body affected. Later there are localized residuals. For example, the whole right side of the body may be initially affected, but after a few days, perhaps just the right arm remains paralyzed. Serious brain malfunctions occur with stroke. Some of them are temporary. The ability to listen, understand or speak may be damaged, but some functions may return. Some may be permanently lost. In addition, over a period of time the brain can substitute functions and some parts can take over and do two jobs for other parts.

Let's look at the comparison between severe intoxication with alcohol or other drugs, especially the sedative-hypnotics, and someone having a stroke. Mild to moderate overdose with the stimulants, such as cocaine, would not appear this way. Extreme overdose with stimulants can manifest the same symptoms as a stroke victim.

Each episode takes away from the top functions with which the brain was born — reserves usually save the individual from obvious malfunctions for long periods of time. The reserve power of the brain is amazing. However, at

**COMPARISONS**

| Compare | Compare |
|---|---|
| ***Alcohol/Tranquilizers/ Sedatives*** | ***Stroke*** |
| Slowed speech | Slowed speech |
| Thick speech | Thick speech |
| Lost eye contact | Lost eye contact |
| Staggering gait | Staggering gait |
| Flat emotions | Flat emotions |
| Frustration in communicating | Frustration in communicating |
| Repetitiveness | Repetitiveness |
| Temporary but later permanent brain damage | Immediate permanent or temporary brain damage |

any given time no one knows how much brain reserve is left. Even after recovery, no one knows unless it is totally gone and then everyone knows.

## Toxic Characteristics

Toxic agents affect the delicate chemistry of a normally functioning brain. Thickened speech, staggering and muddled thinking become the source of entertainment and laughter and derision. The "hit of the party" is the person who cannot pronounce words properly, who staggers, who is flirtatious and loose, who perceives the world around them through blurry eyes and toxic senses, who has high energy and a flight of ideas, a short attention span and who comes up with the unexpected and the absurd to provide entertainment to the others. The scene is not funny, really. The scene is especially unfunny to a spouse, a partner or particularly a child of someone with an intoxicated (poisoned) brain. It's frightening, perplexing and frustrating as it occurs again and again.

Joel Goodman, Ph.D., a psychologist who specializes in the healing aspects of humor, states, "Don't describe anything 'humorous' about the characteristics of another individual unless it can be changed in the next five minutes." Alcoholics and drug addicts cannot change the way their disease is affecting them in five minutes. Nor can a diabetic stop urinating sugar in five minutes . . . without help.

With early toxicity of the brain, losses are almost imperceptible. So many people show early brain toxicity from using drugs and alcohol in our society that even the most severe cases are not "all that different." We don't realize that the effects of the drugs on their bodies are truly toxic damage to their delicate brain tissue.

**Inhibition Loss**

One of the earliest effects is that of loss of inhibition. Many people use mind- and mood-altering drugs for exactly this effect. Their inhibitions are painful and restrictive to them, except when they are on these person-altering chemicals. The Self-Medicator is medicating for assertiveness and the simultaneous loss of inhibition. The person becomes totally self-interested. Immediate gratification is demanded. A clue that someone is under the influence of drugs or alcohol is their lack of concern and consideration for others.

In society we have to live together. We all make attempts and, in fact, go to great efforts to be considerate of one another. We develop a sense to keep us from being inconsiderate. This sense keeps us "tuned in" as to how we are doing with our family, friends and associates. Some of those extra senses we use to ring an alarm for us, when we have ignored or not noticed signals that we are being inconsiderate, are quite delicate and precise and only come with experience and practice. An example might be the ability to see "out of the corner of our eye" and detect the effect our behavior or words is having on someone. This can be seen and felt, even though we are not looking at them directly. Or there is our ability to "hear between the lines" from someone's tone of voice and speech pattern.

We benefit from this information we receive and can continue our negotiations with a much better sense of them and chance for success. We finely tune some of our senses, so we know when we are treading on someone else's toes. These sensitive abilities allow us to be less aggressive than were our forefathers millions of years ago. These extraordinarily developed senses might be considered super-high-frequency antennas that allow us to be more aware of our effect on our world and its effect on us. Why do we have such highly developed senses? Survival — physical, emotional and social.

This extraordinary sense, this specialized ability, is one of the first things dissolved by alcohol or dampened by drugs. Alcoholics and addicts are frequently noticed when they become inconsiderate and don't seem to be aware of their effect on others. Nor do they seem to hear reactions around them or have any sense of any anger or resentment that they may have initiated. Their assertive behavior is frequently mixed with a good deal of grandiosity. It is the medicating effects and the uninhibiting effects of chemicals that lead to perceptions of omnipotence and grandiosity. There is a loss of alertness then, and those circuits in the brain which seem to deal with logic based on information being received are disconnected or temporarily short-circuited. All of these are delicate functions of the cerebral cortex.

### Speech Deterioration

As the drugs or alcohol move through the brain and arrive in increased concentrations in its back section, certain gross events begin to occur. Among them are loss of coordination and difficulty with balance and gait. Sedating influences begin a generalized slowing down of both physical and thought processes. There is a loss of alertness, drooping of the lids and a slowing of the speech. The alcoholic/addict now appears as drunk or loaded. If this particular alcoholic or addict is "loaded at a party again," then it is not too long before they are known as the party drunk.

While all of this is taking place, one of the most highly coordinated, complicated and sophisticated functions of the body begins to deteriorate. This deterioration involves the diaphragm, the lungs, the throat, the larynx, the teeth, the cheeks and the tongue. This vital function is *speech.* Precise speech obediently follows precise thought in its decay under the influence of mind- and mood-altering chemicals. Then as the toxic effects increase, eye-hand coordination, reaction time and reflexes are all affected.

> "Ouch! Sometimes after I've been with you I have such headaches. I feel so shaky and just dead beat. I don't think it's that we stay out all night, stay up late, it's more than that. My muscles are weak. Oh well. I'll tell you, I was sort of uninhibited with you last night. I think they kind of noticed. In a way I had a ball and in another way I am amazed at how uncoordinated I can be with you on occasion. I literally lost my balance on the dance floor. When you are with me, I notice that I have that difficulty, and did you notice me on the tape recording? It was only slight, but I couldn't believe all my 's's' sounded like 'sh's' and I really wasn't making too much sense."

Can you imagine a person who has no peripheral vision or peripheral hearing or peripheral senses, has slowed reaction time, has poor eye-hand coordination, poor balance, sedated with slower thought processes driving behind the wheel of a 2500-pound automobile? The combination of that driver and that vehicle represents a two and one-half ton unconcealed weapon aimed at self and others.

It becomes obvious, then, that with continued drinking there is progression towards more and more toxicity with each drinking episode. As a person uses more and more of a drug or alcohol, their brain becomes more and more poisoned. As a person more frequently uses their chemical to excess, instances of serious brain poisoning increase. Not only do increasing amounts but increasing frequencies of use result in more and more serious conditions.

## Loss Of Choice

So early on brain toxicity provides us with the typical picture of someone who is loaded or drunk. As toxicity progresses, the costs of obtaining and maintaining some sort of chemical state increase. These are not only monetary costs. One of the major costs, actually a loss, that arises as the "party drunk" or the recreational drug abuser proceeds into the toxic phases of their disease is the Loss of Choice.

On any given occasion when alcoholics or addicts begin to drink or use, they cannot choose how much they will drink or use or what their behavior will be. They also lose their choice over how often they will get into drinking and using episodes. When they take their first dose or drink or hit, they might as well say to themselves, "I don't know what is going to happen tonight . . .," but they don't say that. Their denial prevents this. Instead they say, "I can handle it. I'll be careful and just get a little buzz on this time . . ."

> "You know, I'm having trouble really being able to plan on how long we are going to stay out or how often we are going to go out or what we are going to do when we are out together. I really have to tell you that when I first got together with you and couldn't predict what in the world was going to happen, it was kind of exciting. But now it is getting to be kind of a worry for me. And others have said the same thing to me . . . oh well."

Most of us have some control or choice over our reaction to the events in our life from day to day, and certainly from hour to hour. Once alcoholics or addicts begin their use, they lose their right to choose. There is no way they can predict on any given occasion of using or drinking just what will happen. This is the basis for the broken promises to a spouse, who then feels lied to and betrayed.

It is the unpredictability and loss of choice of behavior from using, which results in the accusation, "I never know what to expect from you! You're like a Jekyll and Hyde personality!"

These shifts in personality can be sudden. Unbeknownst to many around the addicted person, there are also frequent changes in personality and reactions that would never be consciously chosen. However, under the influence of drugs or alcohol their reactions seem perfectly justified to them. Often to the intoxicated person, the world is not turning as it should and the people in it are far from acceptable. With early toxic effects, the addict/alcoholic would not necessarily feel this way during periods of abstinence. However, as the disease progresses, this kind of toxic effect on the brain extends even into periods of abstinence. And so, "I never know what to expect from you!" can be elicited even between using episodes.

**Psychological Symptoms**

Psychological symptoms begin appearing. They are more than just anxiety over the supply that the Lover may have, more serious and deeper than the original feelings for which the Self-Medicator was prescribing. Psychological symptoms appear with or between episodes of using or drinking. Many people suffer from the all-American hangover, withdrawal from high toxic amounts. Symptoms include headache or tremors, malaise, depression and anxiety. There is also an ongoing, judgmental, resentful and disgruntled demeanor. Impulsive activity becomes commonplace. The person is obsessed with ideas outwardly and with their drug/alcohol use inwardly. They begin to suspect, sometimes rightly so, that people around them are going to try to separate them and their chemical choice.

> "How do I feel? I'll tell you how I feel! If school was different or if the kids were better, and that damn job and that stupid boss of mine, brother . . . it seems like the whole world is screwed up. I'll change jobs. Yeah! And if that doesn't work, I'll change again. Yeah! I think I'll sell my fishing gear. Those guys are boring me to death and I'll be damned if I'm going back to the club. Seems like only three or four of the guys are really with it and know how to have fun anymore.
>
> "I'm not sure about my wife. There's something wrong. I'm going to start checking on phone calls. I'm going to check distances on the speedometer. I'm going to ask some friends

straight out, got to change things. This is just too much. I'm supposed to be working and all day long I've got my worries at work and trying to keep this home together while at the same time wondering what's happening. I wonder if there is an affair going on. I wonder . . .

"People are out to get me. Let's see, if I stop and write it down on paper . . . Number one, there is a guy at work who would love to have my job. And I'm not too sure the boss doesn't like him better than me. Number two, it is obvious they don't need me around the church anymore, so that's over. I knew that would happen. Number three, I wonder who those folks are who moved in across the street. I don't like the way they look at me when I drive out in the morning. Number four, some of the things I am doing are really on the border, right on the edge. I have a feeling somebody is going to turn me in to the authorities. Number five, somebody in our party group is a fink . . ."

The depression following a cocaine high can be severe and deep. Many attempt to numb its effect with alcohol or to erase it by more cocaine use. Impaired memory, learning, spatial projection (that is, being able to visualize nonvisual aspects of a structure or a landscape), depth perception and coordination do not necessarily return to 100 percent function between bouts of drinking and using.

## Blackouts

Now we are dealing with a brain that is toxic both during use and between uses and becomes even more toxic as each using event occurs. One of the most serious toxic effects is that of *blackouts.*

Blackouts can occur with the use of alcohol or drugs, especially sedative-hypnotic drugs. They can be either partial or complete. They represent amnesia. They are not a condition of passing out, although many people may drink enough to do even that with a blackout. They are a condition of partial loss or complete loss of memory for the events that occurred during the period of use.

The day following a blackout, addicts and alcoholics become quite adept at determining what occurred the night before. They do this by careful questioning of those who were with them. They become adept at covering up the fact that they have a loss of memory, a blank for a certain period of time during their use. This is quite frightening to them. It is frightening and indeed should be, as it represents a major glitch in the delicate functioning of a person's brain. Many times these events are so unrecallable that they become the source of extended arguments the following day. Accusations of lying and alibiing are made. There are times when the evidence becomes irrefutable. "How could you not remember?"

When a person stands on the rug in a pool of their own urine and yet there is no recall of the bladder emptying, or when the car is not in the garage or, worse yet, in the garage with a bent fender and there is no memory of sound or impact, or when the house or family members show the evidence of physical abuse and there is no recall, blackouts have occurred.

In addition to being partial or complete, blackouts can also be short-lived or quite extended. Some alcoholic patients reveal that their blackouts have extended over a significant number of days. Other times blackouts seem to last only for a few hours or part of an hour. These can include incidents such as pilots flying on instruments with no recall or anesthesiologists putting a patient to sleep and waking up in the middle of a surgical procedure not knowing how they got to the operating room. "How did I get home last night?" or "Where did we have dinner last night and what did I eat?" are not unusual questions for an alcoholic/addict to ask. Be sure, however, they ask only themselves.

> "I've got to tell you something. I am so depressed. I know, it is getting worse, even when I am with you. Before, you used to lift my depression so well. But now I'm even seriously depressed between times. I am depressed now when we are together. I think it is the worst I have ever had. It seems to be heaviest right after we have separated, I think. You know, that's another thing, I can't seem to remember things as well. I think I have it down and then, boy, within just a few minutes I've forgotten. Like, some of the things that my spouse and my family

have told me I've done, I just know I haven't. Sometimes my memory is so bad, and I seem to have had . . . like amnesia, that I wonder if I have a brain problem, like a little stroke or a tumor or something.

"Oh . . . I can't let them know I have absolutely no idea what you and I did last night, where we went or what we ate and I didn't understand that phone call this morning. That guy was irate. I don't remember having any kind of a set-to with him or with his wife. I am going to have to find out carefully what went on."

Another loss of choice symptom and sign resulting from the effect of high doses of drugs on our brain is that the person cannot *not* use or drink. There is hardly an alcoholic or addict in the world who has not believed that if absolutely necessary they could control their drinking and use. There is hardly an alcoholic/addict in the world who has not attempted abstinence, maybe on many occasions, and yet they continue to fail, with many justifications being offered for the failure. This is different from simply changing drinking and using styles or occasions. Those changes are made for convenience to prevent detection or adverse consequences and to ensure future use.

Persons who "go on the wagon," "give up dope" or "take a pledge" have an extremely difficult road ahead of them. It can seldom be done without help, frequently professional help. Those who attempt to abstain and fail again and again are fighting their own brain toxicity. And yet they believe that eventually, if they really have to, they can either control or stop their use. Although it might be hard to do, they can quit if they want to badly enough.

Addicts don't realize that people who have no difficulties with drugs or alcohol have no difficulty with abstaining. Persons who have never become addicted to alcohol or drugs have little emotional investment in whether they use or not. The major impact of abstaining from alcohol for a social drinker is that abstaining just doesn't quite fit the social norm of drinking in many areas of our country. (That social norm has changed greatly in the last few years. It used to be common to exclude a person who did not drink from a cocktail party. Now soft drinks and coffee and punches are more socially acceptable, as is the abstainer.)

Someone who has no difficulty with alcohol or drugs has no difficulty with abstaining. Abstinence failure, especially repeated abstinence failure, is a significant symptom of chemical dependency.

> "This is frightening and I . . . I told them all I wouldn't see you so much. I told them all I wouldn't see you at all! Of course, I don't really know if that's true or if I can do it. Remember, I told you once before I tried not to see you. I guess I don't really want to stop seeing you, but I am scared that maybe I can't stop seeing you. I told you that before, too. I knew a guy once that stayed away from you, he said he had the same problem. He was dating you real steady and everybody said stop. So he stopped. He actually stopped for two years like he promised and the minute the two years was up, you and he were back together again. Good Lord! Two years without being with you. I can't imagine what that would be like. I still think that if I really . . . really . . . had to, I could stop seeing you . . . I think . . ."

**Chemical Dependency Symptoms And Signs**

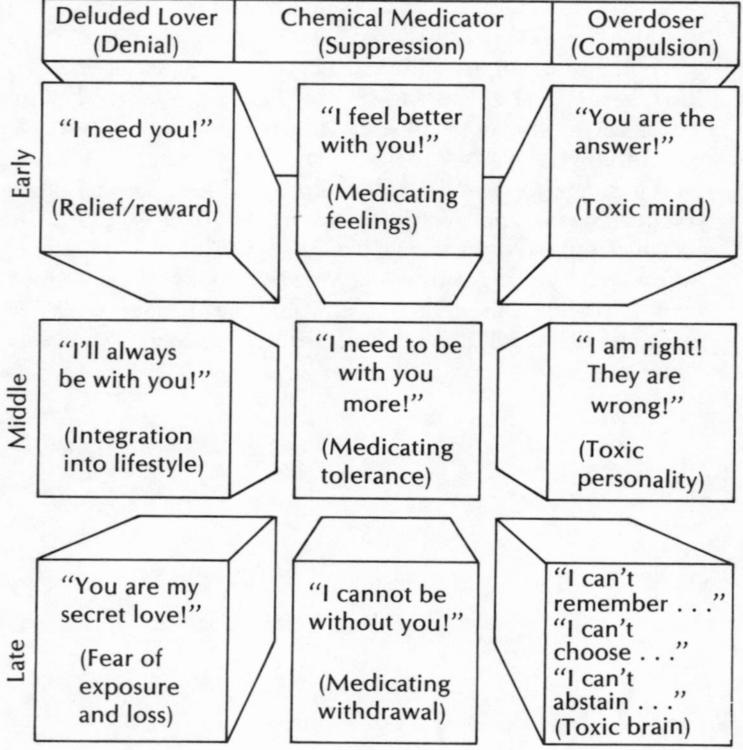


This is a description of the ***PRIMARY*** disease of chemical dependency, showing the major symptom groups that result from the disease affecting the person's ***BRAIN.***

# 4

# Spiritual Complications

## The Loner

Now it becomes necessary to mention the spiritual part of our lives. This is an area individuals tend to withhold from outside observation. And they may even avoid looking inside themselves to get in touch with it.

In examining spirituality, we're not talking about religion. We are talking about that aspect of us which seems to keep us going, gives us energy for each new day and gives us the gratitude expressed when we say, "It's just great to be alive!" The spiritual part of our lives is probably best described as that in which we feel most connected, centered and anchored. We are connected not only to ourself and our child within, but connected to nature and our total environment. We are connected to others and perhaps a special other, and we recognize that there is a power outside ourselves that provides us with life. Some individuals call this power outside themselves God. Others choose to use the words Higher Power.

Connectedness and belonging are basic ingredients of our spirituality. Life is a struggle in which we attempt to survive by fight or flight while we connect, belong and love. Spirituality consists of such things as self-worth, faith, alertness, availability, risk-taking, openness, energy, a low index of expectation, a high index of gratitude, curiosity, hope and perseverance.

These are the characteristics of the indomitable, young, exploring, happy child who we adults continue to search for, yearn for and envy in others. The fortunate ones learn that all those characteristics are still within them and only need reactivating. But in the chemically dependent individual, reactivation comes hard; and it is intermittent and short-lived unless true recovery occurs. Instead, the loss of these characteristics accelerates until the ultimate in spiritual loss occurs . . . the time when a desire to live is no longer present.

Over the years there have been arguments as to what comes first with this disease. Does the spiritual disconnection come after the disease of chemical dependency as one of its complications? Or are emotional, spiritual and psychological problems so intertwined that the primary event in this disease cannot be separated out?

It is important to distinguish between the symptoms of the disease and its complications. This is stressed in *Essentials for the Diagnosis of Chemical Dependency* by Robert and Mary McAuliffe and in *From Social Drinking to Alcoholism* by Dr. Jorge Valles. Many of the symptoms the McAuliffes list are actually problems in the life of the individual with the disease. Some are secondary to having the disease and some do not require the presence of chemical dependency before they appear.

Let's clarify this by looking at the complications that may arise from prolonged use of mind-altering chemicals.

## Complications Categories

There are three major categories, which do not necessarily occur in sequence:

***Spiritual Complications*** — These are the events and problems that arise in a person's spiritual life. They are best described as a "spiritual disconnect." The person becomes a *Loner.*

***Social Complications*** — These are environmental wars in which the person becomes an adversary to family, to job, to friends and to society. This is the *Warrior.*

***Physical Complications*** — We see a quick aging process in which someone, who previously had a most valuable and perfect body, now begins to age rapidly and at a young age becomes a young *Relic.*

Do these complications occur with "recreational use" and "mind-expanding use" of chemicals including alcohol? Yes, spiritual disconnect can accompany that kind of use. Spiritual problems can arise with the use of mind-altering chemicals, even when the actual disease of chemical dependency is not present but chemical abuse is occurring. These problems are usually of lesser degree than those which accompany addiction, and they remain at somewhat the same level, rather than progressing with the disease.

## Spiritual Separation

In untreated chemical dependency, spiritual complications are those progressive, painful, vague spiritual desires and aloneness that set the alcoholic/addict's inner being into more and more disarray. Sensitivities and alertness to reality and the surrounding environment diminish, while self-centered, judgmental, disgruntled attitudes rapidly become a part of the daily pattern.

The changes and effects in the chemically dependent person are different from those of the social, recreational, mind-expanding users who become temporarily diverted from their spirituality. The alcoholic/addict seems to totally divorce from spirituality on what appears to be a permanent basis. To make matters worse, the addict/alcoholic becomes progressively distant from *all* types of connectedness.

The ultimate separation from self, nature, others and a Higher Power, with a total loss of energy for life, comes at the moment of suicide. Suicide may be sudden, impulsive and associated with intoxication. Or it may be sudden, planned and associated with a painful period of abstinence. Or it may be a slow suicide set in motion by a *decision* to capitulate, surrender to the drug. Early on, and perhaps not even noticed, the addict/alcoholic begins to demonstrate a diminished spirituality as shown by increasing self-pity and feeling misunderstood and inadequate. Less interest in others is soon followed by less interest in their own hobbies, negative pessimistic thoughts, a loss of zest and ambition, a loss of outside interests and regrets and feelings of being unique in all of this.

Being prideful, the addict begins to disapprove of others and carry resentments longer than ever before. As the disease progresses into its middle stages, the person is unable to recapture spirituality. Then low self-worth comes into full bloom and is covered by grandiosity and sarcastically putting others down. As the person becomes more judgmental, self-centeredness increases, self-affirmations decrease and there is a disconnect from friends and loved ones.

Then comes a loss of humor, an ethical deterioration and a compromised moral code. Guilt appears and requires much medicating. Put-down humor intensifies and may be accompanied by inconsiderate behavior and thoughts. The person has now become intolerant, cynical and selfish. But although those around him may not see it, he disapproves of himself more than anyone else.

As the later stages of the spiritual complications begin to appear, we see a totally lost spirituality, a sense of worthlessness, a person who is unaware of his or her environment, who is feeling hopeless. This feeling of hopelessness is accompanied by an inability to accept help. And the loss of joy and humor is shown by an almost constant sadness. The person is now suffering from an extreme case of hunger . . . spiritual hunger. Lonely even in a crowd, the person has lost basic beliefs, suffers from shame and is finally plunged into desperation, remorse and despair, which lead to the loss of interest in living. Chemical dependency can be fatal.

By the time people are in love and having an illicit affair with a chemical and become their own physician and pharmacist, they are regularly overdosing with that chemical and their life has become very complicated. They have become hypochondriacs and are preoccupied with the physical self. This separates them from reality even more. Having moved through uninformed, deluded and desperate denial, now they expand their denial to exclude the entire outside world and its reality. As these people talk to themselves, going through their own "headworld" alone but in constant communication with themselves, they might talk about their spiritual complications like this:

> "Life is a bitch. And those people who don't think it is are stupid. I have never had so much difficulty trying to get people to understand. I have thought and thought about what I could do. I'm worried about me. I'm sure I have more to offer in life than what's coming around. Maybe I'm not good enough. Maybe if I could get people to be nicer to me. No, that wouldn't work anyway. And nobody would really understand.
>
> "I don't know what I'm going to do with me. I'll tell you, I don't know why I ever thought I'd be interested in some of that stuff that I got into. I'm glad I just quit. Lord, I'll never bowl again. Stupid game. And I can't imagine why I ever thought I got such enjoyment out of building model airplanes and volunteering down at the shelter. Nobody appreciated me.
>
> "You know, I feel bad that I didn't get a better start in life. I'm sorry I didn't take that job in Chicago and I don't know, maybe I'm even sorry I . . . I don't know. I wish people appreciated what I really have to offer. There's not a one of them, not a one of them that is probably worth my time of day. And I'm ticked off that they don't recognize what I've got to offer . . ."

These inner conversations may go on for years, almost without an individual being aware of them. If they could stop and feel, they would know what a stomachful of negativity feels like. But even that becomes such a normal feeling and so easily medicated away that it is of no consequence. And as the spiritual disconnect gapes wider and wider, the split between low self-worth, grandiosity, hopelessness and self-recrimination increases. Listen . . .

> "I wonder why they won't do it my way. I won't go unless they go with me. It won't matter, I don't need them anyway. In fact, I may get someone else. I may want to get something going, who knows. God knows I need some strokes, and I think I'm justified in getting them wherever I can get them. God, I feel awful about the last time I did that though. But, damn it, what's fair is fair. God, I hope nobody ever saw me. I mean, that kid of mine, Jack the Jerk, probably wouldn't know the difference or suspect, but, boy, would my daughter pick up on it. What am I talking about? I've waited a half an hour, I'm not going to wait anymore.
>
> "I wonder if I need help. No, man, I'll tell you, I don't know what I used to think was so great about this life. Those jerks are going to church this morning. I used to think that did me so much good. God, how can I be so stupid?! Damn, I want something! What is it? I don't think it matters. I am so upset . . . I feel so bad . . . Isn't there someone on this earth meant just for me, that can help ME? I don't care what happens . . ."

Spiritual problems occur from time to time in all our lives. In chemical dependency, they initially occur subtly, yet predictably and devastatingly. In many cases the appearance of social and physical problems also associated with the chemical use become increasingly unimportant to the noncaring addict/alcoholic. The family may feel more helpless, perplexed, unbelieving, angry and paralyzed.

### The Disconnected Family

The family does little while waiting for the spontaneous reversal of a disease process possessing all the power of a runaway locomotive. The symptoms and signs, and even the spiritual complications, are in place and unattended to. It's only when family, job, legal, financial and physical problems arise that it becomes obvious chemical dependency has won a long delaying action which makes the intervention more difficult and the recovery more complicated.

We have not learned to see what we are looking at when we look into the eyes of someone with chemical dependency complicated by a total spiritual disconnect. If we knew how to listen to those eyes and they knew how to talk, they might tell us that the brain they send information to no longer cares for us or our world. If the bottom line could be known, we would also realize that the impaired person's brain may not care about its own inner isolated world.

We wouldn't want to believe this, and early on we would not believe it because we might be misled by sudden bursts of activity in which the alcoholic or addict becomes totally generous and seems interested in the world. But these episodes become less frequent and more short-lived. The ongoing spiritual complications of chemical dependency deepen into chronically low self-worth, isolation, loss of zest for life, becoming disgruntled, acting judgmental and despairing of life ever being any different.

In a letter to Bill Wilson, the co-founder of Alcoholics Anonymous, Dr. Carl Jung, M.D., wrote in January of 1961:

> ". . . the craving for alcohol is the equivalent, on a low level, of the *spiritual thirst* of our being for wholeness, connectedness, the union with God. Expressed in medieval language: 'As the hart panteth after the water brooks, so panteth my soul after thee, O God!', Psalm 42:1."

Spiritual cravings and yearnings, left unattended, require regular medication. On occasion, total anesthesia is needed to quiet the pain. So a cycle of spiritual deterioration gradually turns into a downward spiral. Chronic use of drugs and alcohol results in a loss of spirituality, which requires spiritual medicating with drugs and alcohol . . . which results in further spiritual loss . . . which requires further medicating . . . and so forth . . . and so forth.

## Chemical Dependency Complications

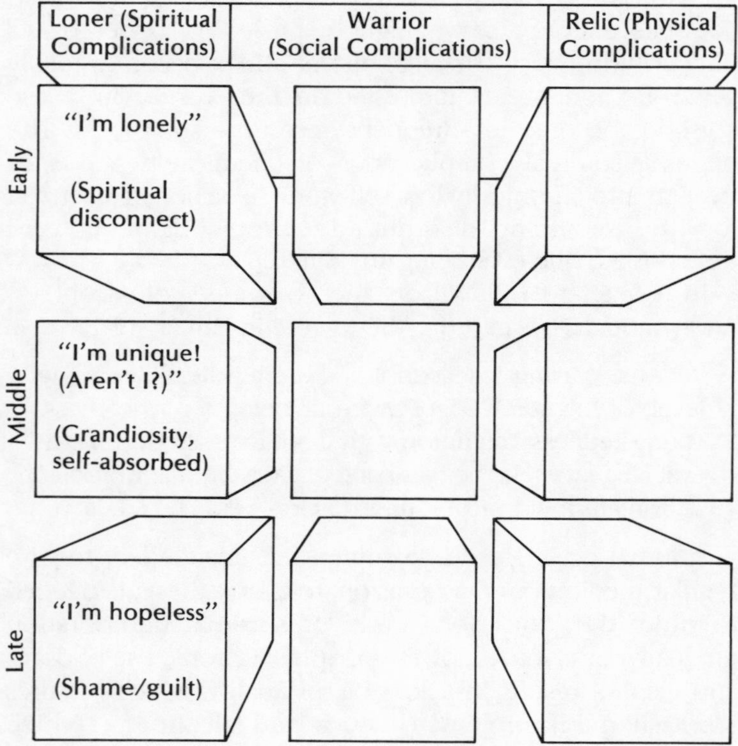


This is a description of the ***RESULT*** of having the primary brain disease of chemical dependency which is allowed to progress to secondary complications that affect the patient's ***LIFE.***

# 5

# Social Complications

## The Warrior

Our bodies, commanded by our brains, can be put on alert in an instant. That alert is the Alarm Reaction that prepares us to fight or flee. Dr. Hans Selye wrote extensively throughout his life on this concept. The Alarm Reaction is the body's ability to instantaneously get ready to stand ground and fight off a saber-toothed tiger, an opponent in a lawsuit or the person on the other side of the tennis net. The opposite of that "fight" alarm is the "flight" alarm, which is the body's ability to instantaneously get ready to flee in the interest of self-preservation.

The heart rate and respiratory rate increase. The amount of oxygen going to the muscles is increased. The muscles tense. And all senses become hypervigilant. As we pass through any given day, we use these defense mechanisms many times over. Although we graciously and outwardly restrain our alarm on most occasions, we all have been inwardly at war with our social environment from time to time. That environment consists mainly of our family life, our social life, our occupational life, our legal life and our financial life.

For addicts or alcoholics well into their disease and already suffering Spiritual Complications, Chronic Overdosing, Self-Medicating and maintaining an Illicit Affair with a chemical, war with their social environment is unavoidable and continuous. And this war exists *during* and *between* drinking and using episodes.

The increasing pain that accompanies Spiritual and Social Complications can be temporarily eased by using alcohol or drugs. Even though the emotional pain is only lessened for a few hours out of each 24, the alcoholic/addict eagerly and repeatedly seeks even this temporary relief. The cycle of use . . . withdrawal . . . use . . . withdrawal . . . becomes entrenched, ingrained, encoded and imprinted.

### Environmental Wars

Environmental wars usually start at home with the family, as problems frequently exist between addict/alcoholic and spouse, even before the kids become directly involved. We often hear it stated that even when a blatant affair is going on, the "spouse is the last to know . . ." In the disease of alcoholism and addiction, the spouse is the first to deny and the last to act.

Another reason a spouse may be *the* last to act is that she or he may have a definite investment in her or his spouse not being "labeled." It might lead to removal from a sensitive position, a position of prestige or high income. It might also mean that the nonaffected spouse is not willing to consider giving up her or his own use of chemicals or lifestyle.

Also the nonaddicted spouse may fear that the partner's sobriety would threaten established positions of power.

A frequent ***sequence of arguments*** put forth by the spouse of the user is:

*First:* "Something's wrong . . . a lot is wrong."
"Something's wrong and it's our marriage."
"Something's wrong, therefore, you drink too much."

*Later:* "Something is wrong with our marriage and it's you and me."
"Something is wrong with us."

*Later:* "Something is wrong with our marriage and your drinking makes it worse."
"Something is wrong with your drinking."

*Later:* "Something is wrong with . . . drinking . . . for you . . . for us, for our marriage."

Changes for the worse can come slowly. This dialogue of awareness may take 10 to 20 years to complete. In the interim, much of the discomfort and behavior has seemed normal until it is reviewed in its entirety.

The disease is so rampant, with subtle but constantly changing behaviors, that the focus is on the individual's behavior rather than any suspected disease. In our society where using and drinking are so universal, chronic interpersonal relationship problems, social problems, job problems or financial problems are not usually linked to the possibility that the individual might have a disease. Instead they are considered living and behavioral problems that are sometimes worsened by a drinking or using period.

**Identifying The Cause Of Social Complications**

The spouse, the user and members of society frequently look upon the social complications of chemical dependency as a *cause,* rather than as a *result* of the using or drinking. People seem to be slow to consider that problems in a marriage, at work, with friends, legally or even financial mismanagement could result from a chronically medicated and overdosed brain. Most of the time we assume that the individual uses or drinks *because* of marital problems or because there is trouble at work, or there is difficulty getting along financially or legally.

One of the major benefits of recovery from alcoholism or drug addiction is that many of the social complications spontaneously disappear. And the recovering alcoholic/

addict becomes adept at solving or working through those that remain, including marital problems.

The spiritual complications suffered by the user and described in the previous chapter do not go unnoticed or unfelt. Those closest to the alcoholic and addict are the first to know something is amiss. Although they can't put their finger on it, there is something wrong. Communication is lessened, predictability is gone and even when the effects of this are slight, family members begin to feel uneasy and fearful. Communication diminishes, trust is chipped away and predictability becomes less and less frequent. This holds true for the spouse and other close members of an impaired person's family. It includes parents if the alcoholic/addict is still living at home. It includes siblings who withdraw rather than have to take sides with mom and dad against a sister or brother, or take sides with sister and brother against mom and dad. Then there are those who are deeply affected during a most sensitive time of their development. These are the children who reside in a family where alcoholism or drug dependency exists in one or both parents.

## Power Of The Disease

Chemically dependent individuals have power by virtue of having a disease. The power is thrust upon the unsuspecting, unaware and unprotected children as well. If somebody could ask an addict or an alcoholic about that power, the inner thoughts might go like this . . . Listen.

> "I have power over my family? I don't want the power. But I guess I need it. If I didn't have the power and if they really knew me, they would probably be embarrassed . . . or not like me . . . or leave. Actually, I sometimes feel like I know what is best for all of us and they seem to be so resistant! So I guess in the long run, I need and probably should have the power. I love the power . . . but when it comes right down to it, they seem to take more care of me than I do of them.
>
> "I have so much trouble talking to them anymore. They don't seem to talk to each other much either. Also, I think they might have secrets from me. I'm feeling less and less a part of this family.

"I wonder how often I've been embarrassing them. I know they are disappointed when I miss a school event but it just can't be helped. There seems to be a lot less trust among all of us and everybody seems to resist even the simplest idea no matter who suggests it. Everybody seems to want to just stand still.

"And the audacity of that oldest one saying they're not coming home for Christmas this year! They know we always have the turkey and the tree. I still wonder why they eloped and wouldn't let us put on a wedding for them. I promised I wouldn't use before the wedding. Of course, we'd all want to celebrate after.

"Sometimes they drink more than I do and I know one of them is blowing all his dough on coke. Even caught the little one sneaking left-over drinks the other night. I actually think the little bugger was a bit high. Bless his heart! Well, at least none of them are in bad trouble with their drugs.

"With all the drinking I've done, I'm sure glad it hasn't affected the kids. They've had everything they needed. I'll talk to them about it but I'll just wait . . .

Wait till . . . . .
Wait till later . . . . .
Wait till later on . . . . ."

Most alcoholic and addicted families wait until it's either too late or almost too late. Most families don't understand what is going on when they are afflicted with the disease. They don't realize how serious it is. Family members who are the first to be affected by the disease do not realize that this disease has power so great that those who are exposed to it are totally powerless.

How can such a power be explained? How can it be described? How can it be taught to the children? How can it be properly respected? These questions continue to go unanswered, not only in the small family society, but in society as a whole. Social complications extend to neighbors, friends, teammates, fellow church members and those with whom we do business. Complications that result from using and drinking are subtle in terms of our social contacts. Many serious changes occur long before an awareness is reached that certain problems are an outgrowth of continuing alcohol and drug practices.

## Social Interactions

Often an individual or couple will migrate toward those with a similar lifestyle. This is not the kind of migration toward other users and drinkers that occurs when the lover is attempting to go underground to find friends and yet not be detected. Often a person or a couple will restrict themselves to friends and activities where drinking and using is not only accepted but condoned and even encouraged. Many parties include a variety of drinking and using activities. And activities in which there is no drinking and using begin to drop by the wayside or are shunned.

Persons with the disease of addiction or alcoholism must find their own group and, therefore, they start choosing very carefully those social groups that will tolerate their particular style of using or drinking. And as their styles change, they must continue to choose and change their social groups. Frequently, this will mean abandoning those who abstain, abandoning those who do not tolerate excessive use, drunkenness, or being loaded. At this stage of the disease, the choice is easy. *First*, go where there are drugs and alcohol; *secondly*, go where there are people who use drugs and alcohol. The choice may be easy for the alcoholic or addict. But these choices can be quite distasteful and perplexing for those who are around the alcoholic or addict. Those who must, go along or are left out.

## Social Restrictions

As people begin to get deeper and deeper into their addiction, complaints by friends become bothersome and appear unfounded. There is a further restriction of the circle of friends and acquaintances or teammates or neighbors who do not complain. The parties become more prolonged. Events are planned and set for an entire day or weekend of using and drinking. There are fewer and fewer non-drinking and non-using activities. There are wider and wider boundaries as to when drinking and drugging will begin and end.

Other aspects of life, such as family life, occupational life and financial life all become affected. Finally, ultimatums may be made by others so that distancing from them begins. There are fewer intimate contacts. Good friends are dropped. Previous values are changed. Lower social status and less desirable companions may be sought.

The variety of friends and activities drops drastically. Then come drinking and using without a party, without friends, without any particular reason or purpose. The amounts and frequency continue to increase while the effects continue to decrease. But the need stays steady, as long as a supply is available. Individual isolation to protect an illicit affair is one thing, but a family isolating and being isolated by society is a sad consequence of the disease of chemical dependency.

## Job Performance

During the time that family difficulties and social isolation are deepening, there is a significant impact from procrastination, disorganization and unfruitful appointments. Job performance is diminished by poor use of time and vague preoccupations. Frequent cancellations of appointments are customary. Haphazard and impulsive business decisions are common. As the individual gets further into the disease, business activities and procedures are modified to make time for more constant use. All this is to the detriment of job performance. There are many "excused absences," along with diminished efficiency and increased difficulty in getting along with others. Delays and missed deadlines are common in the middle stages.

So there is now a 24-hour cycle of spiritual bankruptcy, family problems, the difficulties maintaining an illicit affair, maintaining proper doses and attempting to overdose. Naturally, as people become more undependable and unproductive, they become unemployable. Even so, this seems to be a source of consternation for the user.

"Why me? What did I do?"

The job losses begin to recur. Resumes show time gaps. Then there is no job at all.

"What's happening to me?" is now a frequent and frustrating question the alcoholic/addict asks.

Someone, who once may have been highly productive, articulate, personable, and energetic, is now unemployable. Someone, who once could put full concentration and talents and skills into a project, is now preoccupied and perturbed at any kind of intrusion into chemical use. In the early stages few work problems are noticed. In the middle stages there are occasions where drinking and using interfere with the job. And eventually complications get to the point where any kind of occupation, job, family or friends seriously interferes with the addiction. At first the drinking and using interfered with the job. In the end the reverse is true.

**Employee Assistance Programs**

One of the arenas in which the disease of chemical dependency has been detected, diagnosed and intervened upon has been at the workplace. Employee assistance counselors are trained to recognize diminishing and changing work performance and are able to intervene with employees suffering from chemical dependency.

Corporate denial, just as spouse denial, family denial and individual denial, has to be broken through. Corporations that recognize chemical dependency at work find that it is much more productive to save trained, skilled employees than to discharge them. Those who are disabled from chemical dependency may now find help at work. In companies where people are recovering and employees are fully aware of management's support, there is a special energy. There is a special motivation that arises from a workplace family feeling. It takes special resources, training and full support from the top for corporate programs to work. But the results will justify the costs.

Many alcoholics, regardless of prior experience, knowledge and skill in managing money, lose this ability as their disease progresses. Grandiosity in spending, buying rounds for the house or heavy tipping is a well-known trait of the heavy-drinking loud fellow at the end of the bar. Poor investment strategy and erratic savings practices are commonplace. The inability to avoid impulse spending and buying is quite common. "I'm sorry" gifts may be purchased out of remorse and guilt or an attempt to make up for time not spent with the family.

During active alcoholism a non-addicted spouse may take over the financial management of the family. Then when the alcoholic is in recovery, the spouse may be reluctant to give up the financial management. There may be concern about relapse and the financial dangers that go with it. There is also the reality that a bit of power goes with handling the family finances.

**Financial Losses**

As addicted people increase spending, especially if they are cocaine addicts, financial crises and catastrophes can occur in a very short period of time — as little as 30 days. Relatives who would normally be aware of the financial condition of the use are taken totally by surprise by the drastic financial changes. Thirty to forty thousand dollars a month is not unusual to support a cocaine addiction. It takes but a few months to bankrupt any upper middle-class American. To maintain an adequate income, there is increased searching for multiple sources of cash. This may lead to dealing, gambling, theft, fencing, procuring or bribery. Even during times of abstinence, the problems of poor financial judgment, errors and impulse remain. And financial disaster looms larger.

Additional financial drain comes from attempts to patch up the results of drinking and using, such as legal problems, family problems and health problems. Guilt often leads to buying and buying and buying. Frequently, income becomes more rapidly diminished if a person's income depends on commissions, tips, fees and royalties. As these diminish, the addiction increases. To maintain the addiction, a lesser lifestyle may be chosen. This may require selling off the family car, increasing the mortgage on the house and cashing insurance policies. Hand-to-mouth financial management and bankruptcy occur frequently.

## Legal Problems

Legal threats and a preoccupation with legal rights and insults, contract difficulties and a vindictive drive for victory in the courts are frequently ignited and fueled by an addiction. They may become an individual's only means of coping. Driving while intoxicated may be part of a series of civil and criminal court cases, losses and sentences. A burdensome and complicated lifestyle accelerates. Marginal activities of some drug usage and dealing, especially cocaine, trace out a fine line between imprisonment and personal freedom. However, neither the cocaine addict nor the alcoholic can see how thin the line has become.

As the addict/alcoholic's life becomes more and more a constant war with family, friends, job, school, courts, bankers, church and community, complaints begin to arise. Complaints come from spouses, children and parents. They come from teachers, coaches, employers, police, attorneys and bankers. And this life of complaints is not what the alcoholic or addict intended. That is why the disease of chemical dependency is labeled as a "cunning," "baffling" and "powerful" in *Alcoholics Anonymous*, the "Big Book" of AA. Never considering their disease as the cause, the individual engaged in environmental wars will ask the following questions . . . "What am I doing in a place like this?" or "How did I get into a situation like this?"

Chemical usage in the form of alcohol or other drugs is seldom considered as a serious life complication by the person who is using. As the progression of the disease worsens, those around the alcoholic or addict may agree on the origin of these numerous problems. But they may not know that an underlying disease exists in a troubled individual. They may simply see a connection between the impaired person's incessant use of mind-altering chemicals. Even then they are hesitant to approach the user with such information.

We noted that the alcoholic/addict's spiritual problems, as typified by the Loner, are simply an *expansion* of problems that everyone has from time to time in their lives. On occasion events expand so slowly as to be almost imperceptible and certainly not identifiable by the addict/alcoholic or family members. However, social complications can occur so quickly that people directly affected by the disease blink their eyes and ask, "What happened?" The alcoholic/addict is the first to ask that question. Listen.

> ". . . I didn't really intend to get married so quickly and so soon but it's okay, in fact, it's probably better. In fact, that's probably what I need. Maybe I can still make it. I'm not really ready to be a parent. I'm really quite afraid. Nobody has ever taught me how. I'll do it just like my parents did and I'll be all right as long as we can agree on things and as long as I don't get too far in over my head.
>
> "I like using and drinking. It's one thing that gives me relief from the day-to-day rigors. And you know the group of people we're meeting as we go along now are wonderful! Some are pretty boring but we've agreed we won't hang around with them, or at least I suggested that. It's neat to be with fun-loving people not squares.
>
> "I hope we didn't keep the kids up last night. I know last weekend was pretty tough on them. They kept wandering out. They don't understand. We've gotta decide how to make them mind better. We've got our friends and we deserve our adult time. We can't devote our entire lives to them. I am really amazed at how much we can party and still manage the next day. I seem to be able to time the parties pretty good so I can manage the next day.
>
> "I keep wondering if the kids overhear or ever peek out at some of our antics. That's why I like to go to other people's houses, although they probably hear us coming home and hear the fights we're having. It's funny, when I use and drink, I get so sexed up but sometimes don't do too well. Wonder why my spouse doesn't feel the same way? I bet if we stopped and wrote

down the title of our arguments it would be over sex, money and who's going to discipline and run this family.

"Nobody ever adds up the number of hours of work I've missed, especially on Monday morning when I couldn't quite make it out of the sack and those on Friday afternoon when the happy hours are starting. Probably doesn't amount to much.

"Thank God for credit cards. I wonder if I'll ever get the balance paid off. The bank loans were originally for a good purpose but now I can't even remember what it was I borrowed the money for. They sometimes get snippy about it but I can't avoid overdrawing my checking account. If that just happens once a month, that's $180 a year! But that's not so much. That speeding ticket didn't help though. But damn it, I had to get to the bank on time.

"Why do I procrastinate so? Why don't I just get at it and get it done? It's got to be perfect, though. What's got me where I am so far is that I've insisted on quality and excellence, and I will continue to insist on quality and excellence, especially as far as the kids are concerned. But I cannot turn anything in. I can't finish reports. I can't even do them comfortably anymore, it seems. I think most of it is from my being so conscientious and wanting to do it right instead of slipshod, like I've had to do on a couple of occasions recently. Not going to let that happen again.

"I wonder why Tom and Ann were selected to run the club party this year. We've done it three years in a row. Lord, it was a blast last year. I thought everybody would want us to do it again. I don't understand. We're the most outgoing couple there. Of course, the spouse doesn't seem to have as much fun anymore. Maybe that's it. Maybe if this partner of mine would just shape up and get back into having fun again, we'd do better. I know I would. Anyway, it's more fun dancing with everyone else now.

"It's funny how the whole world seems to be bitching a lot lately. I really feel like the world sometimes goes on without me. I have to keep my eyes open and stay alert so I don't get left out. I'd have sworn I paid that dealer. I think he might be taking me.

"Thank God, I have a charge account at a couple of liquor stores. At least I can ping-pong them back and forth. We gotta have a higher income. I've got several ideas about that. May have to become a two-job family. To hell with all that. I may have to become a no-family person and a different-job person. In fact, maybe we need a different town.

"Those supposed good friends don't seem to be around so much anymore. And the club can take its membership and shove it! As soon as I figure out how to pay off these debts or split them with the spouse and clear up these legal messes that people are causing us . . . I think I'll split . . . I'll go back home. God, I miss home . . . What am I doing in a fix like this? . . . What am I doing in a job like this? . . . What am I doing in a place like this? . . . What am I doing with people like this? . . ."

**Chemical Dependency Complications**

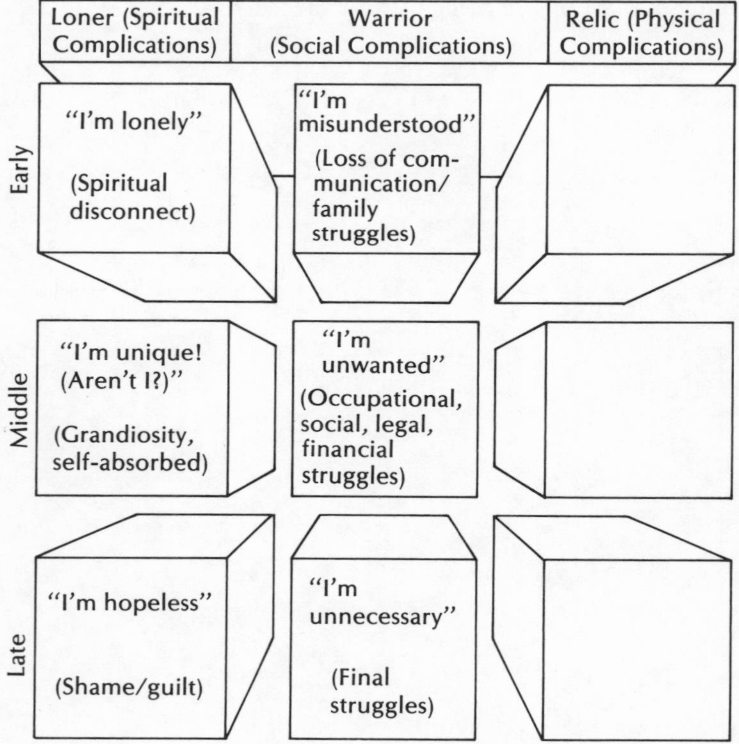


This is a description of the ***RESULT*** of having the primary brain disease of chemical dependency which is allowed to progress to secondary complications that affect the patient's ***LIFE.***

6

# Physical Complications

## The Relic

Ongoing use of mind-altering chemicals, such as cocaine, marijuana and alcohol, results in serious physical consequences. The effects of taking chemicals into the human body can be devastating, whether it is over a period of years or in frequent and large doses. The overall effect of this kind of usage on the human body is best described as a "quick aging process." If a medical student were taught just those processes that occur within the different organs and systems of the body due to chemical use, the student would also understand the impact of age and poor health care on the body.

The human body adapts well, and different bodies adapt in different ways. Physical adaptation can be beneficial. If you play the guitar or use a jackhammer regularly, for example, your hands will develop calluses. Athletes develop cardiac reserve, the ability of the heart to put out more and more work. Weight lifters or laborers can increase muscle mass at the expense of fat and increase their strength.

There are also body adaptations that are destructive, such as the formation of a blister in an area unused to rubbing and steady contact. This results in the death of underlying tissues and is a far cry from the slow, careful adaptation the skin makes when forming a callus. In cardiac failure, the heart actually puts out less work and therefore diminishes the amount of necessary blood flow. The back-up of flow through the vessels results in shortness of breath. Blood is encroaching upon air spaces. Loss of muscle mass comes from sedentary behavior or even bed rest. This results in an influx of fat which replaces muscle tissue and muscle mass.

In addition to the body's positive adaptations and negative reactions, it can also accommodate and incorporate foreign substances into its functioning. This may appear to be non-destructive at first.

For example, the incorporation of a drug, such as nicotine, into the metabolic cycle may seem at first to have no adverse effects other than the accommodation of the metabolic cycle to the substance. However, once all the cells in the body make an accommodation to such substances as nicotine, alcohol and cocaine, the body then "expects" them on a regular basis, in increasing amounts. If these chemicals suddenly stop, the body ceases to function as it has. Uncomfortable, and perhaps serious, withdrawal then follows.

The major effects of withdrawal are on the nervous system, including the brain and the spinal cord. We have previously listed these as primary symptoms and signs of overdosing the brain.

This chapter deals simply with the physical consequences of chronic prolonged use of chemicals on the normal body, its organs and its systems of organs.

It's important to know that the effects of these drugs do not just take place during the time of use or intoxication or being high. The effects of chronic or excessive use of the drugs, including alcohol, are persistent and only diminish with prolonged and consistent abstinence from them. Abstinence may be too late, depending on how far the physical effects have progressed. Some physical effects are irreversible.

## Early Physical Signs

Dentists and dermatologists could diagnose alcoholism sooner than any other medical specialty because of the early and distinct changes in teeth, jaws and skin. Gingivitis, poor dental hygiene, frequent cavities and the effects of excessive smoking on the teeth are apparent to dentists. Dermatologists may look for blemishes, slow healing, bruises and numerous evidences of minor trauma, such as scratches, cuts, nicotine-staining of the fingers and numerous random burns or bruises on the body. Prematurely aging skin and discolorations are also common.

Generalized body changes can be excessive. Water storage causes swelling or edema. Body fat deposition and storage gives the appearance of bloating, "beer belly" and overall pudginess. Those who use cocaine and other "upper" drugs are just the opposite. They suffer from a loss of appetite and the accelerated metabolism associated with hypermanic behavior. Actual appearances of anorexia and food deprivation may appear.

Nutrition problems arise from the preoccupation with drugs and not eating properly, and also from the direct effect of some drugs on vitamin metabolism. The pale face of the teenage grass smoker and lover of acid rock music is a perfect example of skin and nutritional changes.

## Advanced Symptoms

Later in the more advanced stages of chemical dependency, hypertension (high blood pressure), hepatitis (liver inflammation) and insomnia begin. The liver becomes enlarged and tender as abnormal laboratory tests for liver function appear. This may be the very first time a physician says anything to the user about the use of pills, illicit drugs or alcohol.

Most of our information on the effects of chronic mind-altering drug use on the human body comes from studies on abuse of the sedative-hypnotic drug alcohol. However, more and more corroborating information on tranquilizers, sleeping pills and other drugs, such as morphine, Demerol, and codeine, indicates that they may produce equally devastating effects. Heroin, hash and hallucinogenic drugs, such as PCP and LSD, have equally damaging effects on the body, especially the brain. Recently evidence showed that even in the intervals between usages, psychic stimulants, such as the amphetamines and cocaine, can also cause serious and permanent changes in many body systems.

The ingestion of alcohol through the gastrointestinal tract results in a direct effect in that tract. Effects occur in the mouth, stomach, esophagus and intestines, as well as in related organs, such as the liver and pancreas.

### *Liver*

The liver is the most notorious organ of our body in terms of its reaction to the effects of alcohol. The liver is also greatly affected by other mind- and mood-altering chemicals because the liver is the main detoxifying organ in our body. It carries on the workload of ridding our body of many substances and their breakdown products. Other organs of the gastrointestinal system, such as the stomach and intestines, are also easily affected because they are the routes of entry for many of the substances to which people become addicted.

Alcoholics are frequent users of over-the-counter medicines, including antacids, because peptic ulcer disease is common in alcoholics. Alcohol and nicotine make matters worse for people with peptic ulcer disease. And a quick gag reflex is more easily triggered in alcoholics. Early morning withdrawal gagging episodes can even occur while brushing the teeth. When the gag reflex is "anesthetized" by the use of suppressant sedative-hypnotic drugs, such as alcohol, choking episodes may happen. Emergency room and emergency vehicle attendants find that most choking incidents in restaurants occur in those who have been imbibing heavily.

The liver is one of the most damaged organs. Hepatitis is the inflammation, swelling and diminished function of the liver. It can be as serious as infectious hepatitis. Alcoholic or chemical hepatitis is just one of a few of the lesions of the gastrointestinal tract that may occur. Gastritis, esophagitis, esophageal varicose veins and acute ulcers are also common. Chronic bowel syndrome and alternating constipation and diarrhea may show up in the middle stages of the disease.

As the disease progresses, the effects become greater and the liver begins to react to chronic hepatitis and drug use by a process of excess fat infiltration and of hardening or scarring. This latter process is called cirrhosis and can continue for some time before the patient will see a physician. It may even continue for some time after treatment and abstinence have been obtained. Cirrhosis is probably an irreversible process, but can encompass most of the liver without causing death. However, if an alcoholic has to undergo anesthesia, this may result in acute liver failure. Acute liver failure is usually fatal.

### *Pancreas*

Standing alongside the gastrointestinal tract is the pancreas, which is extremely important for producing certain enzymes for digestion. The pancreas also produces insulin to regulate our body and blood sugar levels. Alcoholics may be unable to absorb foodstuffs from their intestines because of the interference with these digestive enzymes. Chronic inflammatory changes in the pancreas, similar to those in the liver, may also occur.

They are usually only relieved by abstinence from the offending toxic chemical. However, acute pancreatitis can be fatal.

With this impact on the gastrointestinal system, it might be suspected that alcohol would interfere with good nutrition. That is indeed the case. Because half of the daily caloric requirements can be met by the intake of alcohol, often an unnoticed nutritional difficiency occurs. The calories provided by the alcohol are "empty" calories, containing none of the vitamins, minerals, amino acids or fatty acids that our bodies require. Addicts abusing chemicals other than alcohol frequently have poor nutrition with the same end result.

### *Malnutrition*

Secondary malnutrition occurs because of alteration of the organs in the gastrointestinal tract. Nutrients are neither digested properly nor absorbed completely. Vitamin A, folic acid, thiamin and vitamin B6 are commonly lowered or absent. Alcohol abuse has been suggested as the most common cause of vitamin deficiency in the United States, according to Dr. Michael J. Eckkert, Ph.D. (*JAMA*, August 2, 1981, Volume 286, No. 8). Both inadequate intake and other factors contribute to this, according to Dr. Eckkert. The results of some vitamin deficiencies are extremely serious, such as Wernieke's brain pathology due to thiamin deficiency. Other nutritional deficiencies include abnormalities in other body functions such as anemia, convulsions and small bowel dysfunction.

Gross tremors, difficulty with fine balance, and slowing of thought processes may result from the use of mind- and mood-altering chemicals. And these can be accompanied by other nervous system changes. In addition to the Wernieke syndrome, whose major symptoms are total confusion, difficulty in focusing the eyes and difficulty with gait, there is also a type of nerve involvement that probably results from the effects of these drugs on the cerebellum which is mainly responsible for balance. If patients with Wernieke's receive proper vitamin B6 therapy, the symptoms often show marked improvement.

Persistent amnesia, which can accompany Wernieke's disease, is called Korsakoff's Psychosis. Although there can be marked improvement in many of the symptoms, there is seldom complete recovery. In fact, some individuals remain passive and indifferent, lacking any emotional response or motivation. Because of this, their difficulty in being able to recognize and remember and their impaired intellectual ability, many of these patients remain in institutions for the rest of their lives.

More and more information is being obtained on brain wave measurement in chemically dependent individuals, both during intoxication and between episodes. It appears that chemically dependent patients can be differentiated from normal subjects. Even offspring from chemically dependent subjects appear to have different brain wave tracings than normal subjects. Numerous investigators have made estimates that brain and nervous system impairment is present in half to three-fourths of alcoholics who enter treatment centers.

Additional effects on brain functioning in chemically dependent people come from malnutrition, repeated head injuries and other medical complications. Other problems are muscle weakness, pain, diminished sensation to touch and strange sensations coming from the extremities. Some of these effects are reversible. In fact, most are if good nutrition and abstinence are undertaken as part of the recovery program.

Delirium tremens is an acute psychotic state of profound confusion and hallucinations such as seeing, smelling, hearing or feeling things that are not actually there. Elevated temperature and pulse, profuse sweating and a coarse tremor involves the entire body, usually occurring two to three days after a chronic period of drinking. Originally, the death rate from delirium tremens was 20% to 25%, but with earlier and vigorous treatment there are fewer fatalities.

### *Holiday Heart Syndrome*

Sydney Cohen, M.D., coined the term "Holiday Heart Syndrome." This is an attractive name for a condition that is neither glamorous nor rare. It is caused by the excessive consumption of alcoholic beverages in a binge with resulting irregularities in heart rate. Since inordinate drinking episodes often occur during holiay celebrations, the term "Holiday Heart Syndrome" naturally evolved. However, it is frequently more than just an unusually large consumption of alcohol that produces irregular heart rates. Cocaine intoxication and other drug overdoses can cause these symptoms. Fast heart rates are quite common. Fluttering heart rates, premature beats and double beats have all been recorded.

Often a patient will feel faint, dizzy and weak during one of these episodes of heart irregularity. Sometimes the only malfunction found in the heart of an addict or alcoholic in the middle stages is a rhythm disturbance. Even though there has been some evidence that small amounts of alcohol may have a beneficial effect on the heart, when it comes to coronary artery disease, it is felt that the harmful effects of large amounts of alcohol on the heart outweigh any of the beneficial effects.

### *High Blood Pressure*

High blood pressure is a major problem that accompanies alcoholism and addiction. It is usually chronic and of the moderately elevated type. But high readings of 220 over 110 can be recorded during a heavy drinking or cocaine episode. Most of the time abstinence for a week from any of the offending drugs will result in normal blood pressure unless the individual has other reasons for the elevated readings. Hypertension in addicts is probably caused by the activation of the sympathetic nervous system by adrenaline-like chemicals the body produces. Adrenaline is well known to increase heart rate, the work of the heart and blood pressure.

Many patients with cancer of the mouth, pharynx, larynx, esophagus and liver are also found to be alcohol dependent. There has been an increased incidence of cancer in these parts of the body because of associated smoking with its damaging direct effect on tissues. It has been calculated by some investigators that 76% of cancer of the mouth, pharynx and larynx would be eliminated if exposure to both alcohol and tobacco were avoided.

Other serious physical complications seen in chemical dependency are accidental or experimental overdosing, sudden intake, seeing who can smoke the most, who can snort the most, who can drink the most. Deaths on a dare are not uncommon. Assault, rape and accidents such as fires, drowning and traffic accidents certainly have their impact on the physical well-being of an individual using alcohol and other drugs.

Runny nose, red and raw nostrils, watering eyes, poor muscle control or abnormally constricted or dilated pupils may indicate drug usage. When a person's pupils are widely dilated in the sunlight or completely constricted in dim light, there is a strong indication that this person is under the influence of a drug.

### *Organ Deterioration*

Due to the physical insult it takes from combined drinking, drugging and smoking, the respiratory tract suffers from frequent pneumonia, chronic laryngitis and pneumonitis. Even when alcoholics are nonsmokers, they have twice the rate of cancer of the lung. They have diminished resistance to other respiratory infections and allergies, and they often have chronic bronchitis. Today the incidence of tuberculosis remains higher in those who are addicted to alcohol and other drugs than it is in the general population.

The physical consequences of the disease of chemical dependency can best be summed up as a "quick-aging process" of the entire body. "Softening," "hardening," "slowing," "discoloring" and "diminishing" are all terms that can be applied to the organ systems of the body following the prolonged effects of alcohol and other mind-altering drugs.

In time the hypochondriac addict begins to show evidence of more than just "imagined" symptoms. There are real, yet seemingly minor, ailments and afflictions. Then come minor to moderate problems which are treated without the basic underlying cause being suspected, diagnosed or treated. The organs begin to function poorly. And as the more advanced, somewhat more directly related diseases occur, attention is given to them because of their life-threatening qualities. But again, the underlying problem is frequently not addressed to the degree that it will ensure there will be no relapse. Because of this, many of the medical problems and complications that occur with chemically dependent individuals happen again and again and again . . . and the organs begin to suffer actual damage. The impaired person's body is truly becoming a Relic.

## Chemical Dependency Complications

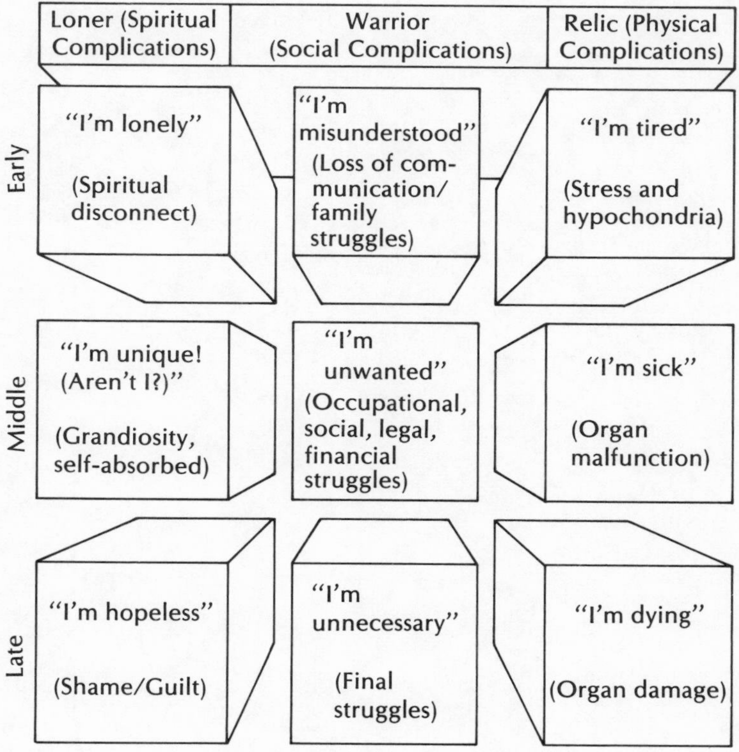


This is a description of the ***RESULTS*** of having the primary brain disease of chemical dependency which is allowed to progress to secondary complications that affect the patient's ***LIFE.***

# 7

# Stages And Severity Of Chemical Dependency

The word "course," as it is used in medicine, means the pathway or usual sequence of events of a disease. Stopping points along the way are designated as early, middle or late stages of the disease.

"Stages" are times in the disease process that we can define and detect fairly clearly. Stages naturally cluster themselves and become relatively well fixed. Although they are an arbitrary designation, they are still useful.

When stages of a disease are distinct enough to be universally accepted, they can be more easily diagnosed and used to predict final outcomes. Those diseases which have distinct stages are more easily taught to students and allow for more effective research by scientists. Most importantly, staging a disease permits a proper choice for therapy and helps determine how long recovery may take. Certainly, staging facilitates more accurate evaluation of our treatment methods and outcomes.

There are points along the course of development of chemical dependency at which various stages can be distinguished. Earlier, when we described signs and symptoms and complications, we described entire categories. For example, early Self-Medicating symptoms were followed by middle- and late-appearing Self-Medicating symptoms. We did not follow the course of the illness as it actually occurs in the individual.

In reality long before Self-Medicators reach the later stages of self-medicating, they are suffering many overdosing symptoms and at least some spiritual complications. By the same token, extreme complications may not show up until long after the appearance of late-stage symptoms and signs. And there are occasions where family and social conflicts appear quite early in the course of an illness.

In general we can state that the early signs and symptoms may appear and stand alone long before any complications arise. That is, a person can learn to medicate feelings and drink for the effect of it, in addition to occasionally becoming intoxicated. Depending on circumstances, this may not lead to complications for a great length of time. However, by the time an individual is into a full-blown Romance with alcohol or drugs and we see Tolerance developing, personality changes are becoming more or less permanent. Almost always some type of complications begin appearing in their life.

In medicine we group complications as to whether they are mild, moderate, severe or extreme. In the case of chemical dependency, there seems to be little room for designating any event as a mild complication. The earliest complications we observe seem to be moderate or severe. Once symptoms and signs indicate the middle stage of disease, individuals are probably well into a Spiritual Disconnect, Family Conflict, Secrecy and Early Aging (moderately severe complications).

Diseases usually increase in severity as they progress along a time scale. That is, the later in the disease, usually the more severe the disease. Signs and symptoms are described in chronological terms such as early, middle and late. Complications are usually characterized in severity terms such as mild, moderate, severe and extremely severe. In either case the more severe or the later the appearance of an event, the more detrimental it is to the individual.

Severity is defined as the risk of death or temporary or permanent impairment from a disease. Stages exist during times of differing severity in a disease process. They are distinct and can be defined and clinically detected. Remembering that the three groupings of symptoms and signs include Lover, Medicator and Overdoser and the three groupings of complications include the Loner, Warrior and Relic, we can proceed through the course of chemical dependency and its various stages.

## Early Stages

Early symptoms and signs of chemical dependency occur as the individual takes on the roles of Deluded Lover, Medicator and Overdoser. Young people experiment with drugs and alcohol. Their curiosity is great. Peer pressure is there to use and to belong.

Experimentation coincides with learning to use. First they use other people's supplies. Then they begin to acquire their own. And a definite relationship has begun.

Substance users quickly learn exactly which medicines are good for energy, fun, assertiveness, sex, etc. They also learn what drugs kill emotional pain. In doing so, they frequently overdose. Sometimes that's even the goal. They set out to poison the brain, get drunk and be high. In some cases episodes of overdosing may occur only every third or fourth time there is drinking and using. In other cases episodes are spaced far apart but always involve an overdose. In either case overdosing is overdosing. It is a toxic condition of the brain.

The early symptoms of chemical dependency exhibited by the Lover, Medicator and Overdoser may go on for some time without complications appearing. If complications do appear, they tend to be transient, minor or situational. The early addict or alcoholic quickly becomes adept at skirting around problems and trouble caused by overdosing.

What about chemical users who become early Lovers, Medicators and occasional Overdosers, yet never seem to go beyond the early stage with their symptoms and problems? Perhaps these are social drinkers or recreational users. It is almost impossible to tell which individuals in the early use of chemicals will cross over the line into full-blown chemical dependency.

However, chemically dependent persons have passed through the early stage and exhibited the symptoms and signs of that stage. On occasion, they have remained in that stage for some time. Quite often, however, you will hear someone say they've been ". . . alcoholic from the first drink." But they will also have demonstrated the symptoms of "I found it" and the same signs of overdosing before proceeding to the middle stage. In the beginning it is difficult to determine who is a social drinker, recreational user or chemically dependent person. But when a person has reached the middle and later stages of symptoms and signs, it becomes less troublesome. Social drinkers simply do not progress to the middle and late stages.

The denial that accompanies the early stages of chemical dependency is usually based on lack of information or misinformation: "It can't hurt me . . . My friends tell me so!" or "I understand if I just drink beer or only smoke grass, I'll never have any problems with drugs." In times of intoxication, denial may be in the form of, "I'm perfectly all right; I can drive perfectly well. I actually perform better when I'm a little high."

## Middle Stages/Moderate Complications

As chemically dependent people begin to incorporate drugs and/or alcohol into their lifestyle, they enter into the middle stages of the disease where little is done without the thought or presence of alcohol or drugs. This is the full-blown Romance for the Lover. There is preoccupation and there are rituals and customs. Alcohol is number one on the Hit Parade. This stage may continue for many years with little thought given to the importance of alcohol and drug use in the home, even though it becomes the keystone of the family. As this goes on for an extended time, dosage problems begin. The Lover is enjoying himself while the Medicator begins to notice there are some changes taking place.

It becomes evident that more is needed. There seems to be less effect. There are times when the individual can't consume it fast enough. They begin to increase the dose by taking extra amounts or using extra strong stuff. Then comes switching and mixing with other drugs or prescription medications. The body's tolerance causes a sense of frustration as the party ends; the user still wants to continue or actually does continue after others have stopped. Often they continue without being discovered.

As the middle stages continue, even for decades, personality changes begin as a result of brain poisoning. Over the years a person may change so radically that they may bring on the accusation of, "You're a Dr. Jekyll and Mr. Hyde when you drink!" A person may be hyper one moment and hypo the next or argumentative and defensive. The previously easygoing person who was able to negotiate may become overbearing and insensitive. People who used to take responsibility for themselves and their feelings may become paranoid and project their own difficulties onto others. People who used to be bright and sharp and successful may become slower mentally and develop an inability to get along with others.

Simple hangovers often occur in the early stages due not only to excessive imbibing or drug use but also to associated activities. Excessive food, late hours, nicotine and vigorous activities all lead to the all-American hangover the following morning. However, the withdrawal symptoms that appear in the middle stages are not due to excess. They are caused by an actual absence of the substance taken in excess at a prior time, usually the evening before. Withdrawal is serious and indicates true tissue addiction.

Tissue addiction means that every cell in an individual's body is accustomed to the presence of the alcohol, other drug, nicotine or even caffeine and has incorporated that substance into its own biochemical machinery. When the drug is suddenly withdrawn, there is great imbalance within the cell's metabolism and every cell in the body responds. Signs and symptoms of withdrawal are confusion, emotional upset, headache, irritability or anxiety, gross tremors or tremors on attempting to reach for something or to write legibly. On occasion these symptoms become so severe that the individual needs to be hospitalized. Usually a person will self-medicate.

The signs and symptoms in middle stages are determined by the Lover incorporating the use of alcohol and drugs completely into his/her life, having a continuous preoccupation and giving chemicals number-one priority. Middle stages include the beginning of tolerance problems, with more needed while less effect is noticed, and stronger and more frequent amounts required by the Medicator and Overdoser. Personality changes and moderate withdrawal symptoms also begin to appear on discontinuation of the substance.

In the middle stages denial seems to be more directly related to effects of mind-altering chemicals on the brain itself. Because ingesting these drugs brings an increased euphoria, and because euphoric recall is so strong following a drinking and using episode, denial stems from the fact that the individual has absolutely no awareness of any danger or difficulty in the use of drugs or alcohol. They are truly deluded.

As personality changes occur, brain chemistry and perhaps even brain structure begin to change. The abilities of insight, logic and perception are markedly diminished. This reinforces the denial. Middle stage delusion and denial continue on and on until events and circumstances change enough for the denial to lose its power. Even then, when overt denial is lost, delusion and denial continue to reside in the innermost recesses of the mind. Outside circumstances, however, continue to chip away at deluded denial until the desperate denial of the late stage of the disease arrives.

As the middle stages of the disease are reached, complications begin to appear. The Lover-Medicator-Overdoser takes on additional roles that add the Loner-Warrior-Relic. The Loner becomes spiritually disconnected. The Warrior begins to have environmental wars with people, places and things. The Relic begins to show physical signs of ongoing chemical dependency. Most of these events occur in succession, but it can be variable.

As the Romance comes into full bloom and Tolerance is developed, spiritual changes take place, too. Often there seems to be a vague desire for something life is not providing. The individual begins to feel lonely even in a crowd. A commonly heard remark at Alcoholics Anonymous meetings is, "I was always alone. No one understood me, even in a bar or at the frat house." Self-pity, lack of motivation and feelings of low self-worth begin to take over as middle stage events and symptoms pile up around the impaired person.

The individual is torn between maintaining the addiction and contending with the outside world. The addict's most vulnerable and available enemy is right at home. Family members are the ones who need to be under control. They are the ones who need to understand. They are the ones who need to shape up. They are the ones who should only speak when spoken to. And they are the ones who are the root of all the problems.

When the family members insist on talking or lack trust or begin to show feelings, war is on. In the middle stages, war may go no further than the house. And the disease may progress for some time before the arrival of the next stage of environmental wars when the impaired person does battle outside the home. And while the Warrior battles, the Warrior also begins to show physical effects.

## Moderate Complications

In the middle stages of the disease, moderate complications start appearing. These include early aging affects, diminished hygiene, poor dental repair, skin changes and a rapid pulse. There can also be skipped heartbeats, difficulty with water retention and bloating. Personality changes, spiritual difficulties and family conflicts are happening along with multiple physical illnesses and hypochondria. There are many visits to the doctor, resulting in no definitive diagnosis.

In the middle stages of the disease while the addict and loved ones are suffering, help is often sought for the wrong reasons because of the denial that alcohol or drugs are at the root of the problems. It is difficult for family therapists to determine that an individual's use of alcohol or drugs is the basis for the problems that are presented. So they frequently take on the role of arbitrator and negotiator between members of the family. Physicians looking at individuals complaining of multiple minor aches and pains will often use trial-and-error prescriptions in an effort to bring relief. The physician is likely to be frustrated with the patients who keep returning with the same problems plus additional complaints. Skin changes, water retention and irregular heartbeat quickly become the focus of a treatment plan and monitoring. And the underlying pathology goes undetected.

It has been commonly taught that alcoholism may take 10 to 20 years to develop in a male; that the disease in the female "telescopes" down to 10 to 12 years and that it may take only one to five years for teenagers to develop the disease. But the differences between sexes and ages may not be as great as prior teachings held. Understanding of the disease concept has changed greatly since the days when chemical dependency was defined as the use of mind- and mood-altering chemicals to a point that interfered with the major areas of an individual's life. That definition utilized complications, rather than symptoms and signs, to describe chemical dependency. So despite symptoms of deterioration, a male may be able to withhold the appearance of complications for maybe decades. But a female has more difficulty, especially with family and social conflicts. And a teenager with few resources to resist the appearance of complications would more quickly display effects of the disease and become obvious.

In summary, middle-stage complications, including spiritual and family conflicts that accompany symptoms and signs, are predictable and if looked for, are detectable. But this requires great cooperation from the family and trust from the individual who is chemically dependent.

## Late Stages/Late Complications

Individuals in the middle stages of chemical dependency are quick to recognize that they are different from others who use drugs and drink alcohol. Because they seem to place greater importance on the use and presence of substances, they notice that they require more and continue consumption longer than others. Also other people are complaining about their behavior. People are noticing their personality changes, too. When this occurs during the course of a Romance with chemicals, the addict knows something has to be changed. The Romance is threatened. Even though the Romance no longer seems totally desirable, there is an urgency to continue it. In the late stages of chemical dependency the Romance must become secret. So the Lover goes underground to begin an illicit affair.

At this stage the Pharmacist is quite busy medicating feelings and maintaining proper dosage. But now there is a third problem to deal with. That problem is the frequency of withdrawal symptoms. And the Overdoser, whose brain-poisoning is becoming more devastating and is triggering destructive personality changes, begins to suffer major losses.

The late stage of chemical dependency is now in place. The Lover suffers the consequences of alienation and isolation that go with secret using and drinking. The Pharmacist, to maintain physical and emotional stability, now starts medicating withdrawal in the morning or even around the clock, depending on need. Then come the final and absolute signs and symptoms of chemical dependency. There is loss of control of amounts used. Behavior becomes almost totally unpredictable. Loss of memory starts. There may be partial or complete blackouts (amnesia). There is a loss of any ability to abstain and severe withdrawal symptoms occur.

These late stages for the Lover-Pharmacist-Overdoser are accompanied by extreme complications suffered by the Loner-Warrior-Relic. There is a loss of faith. Social contacts, including family and society, are lost. Jobs are lost. The body functions poorly and develops problems of the cardiovascular system, stomach, intestines, liver, lungs and hormones. Sexual performance problems are common, too.

The denial that accompanies late-stage symptoms and signs is desperate. In the face of the changes occurring in the individual's life, denial of reality is now more difficult to practice. However, deep in the recesses of the mind of the perplexed alcoholic/addict, there may still be the thought, "If I really have to, I can change things." Even in recovery there are times when sober people get the fleeting thought, "I really don't have any problem with alcohol or drugs." It is amazing how deeply entrenched such an idea can be in the brain of an addict. "If only . . ." and "Yeah, but . . ." or "It isn't as bad as . . ." are all statements of a lingering desperate denial capability.

The Loner and Warrior fall into hopelessness and suicidal tendencies. Common problems at this stage are violence, job-jumping, existing alone and having complicated financial and legal problems. The Relic suffers not only from poor bodily function, but also from actual organ damage. Ulcers, fatty heart, cirrhosis, pancreatitis, DTs, wet brain and serious trauma set the final scene. And if physical death doesn't occur, there is institutionalization and social death in a health facility or a prison.

*Summarizing:* The course of chemical dependency can be described in distinct stages. Early in the course of the disease a person establishes a courtship with chemicals and uses them for minor medication of feelings, as well as to blot out the brain by becoming intoxicated.

In the middle stages, addicted people totally incorporate chemicals into their lifestyle. Chemicals become number one. Tolerance develops, with increasing amounts needed to obtain the same effect. There are toxic effects on the brain that bring personality changes which may be permanent, even in times of non-use. This is accompanied by the appearance of complications, such as a spiritual disconnect, frustration with life, family conflicts, signs of early aging, and perhaps even hypochondria.

In the late stages of the illness, the individual notices that the love affair with a chemical is abnormal. So it goes underground. The illicit affair begins. Now the medicating aspects of the disease are not just for emotional factors, but also for self-detoxification and to gain relief from the withdrawal symptoms following overdosing. The impaired person has almost no choice now over how much to use or drink or what behavior to display. Impulse control has disappeared. Abstaining for even moderate periods of time is hardly possible. And there is usually either partial or complete memory loss when using.

The complications at this stage are now clearly severe. They include feeling hopeless, being judgmental, waging social wars, developing difficulties at work and with friends and having financial and legal difficulties. In the meantime the body is beginning to show the effects of constant use. The severe complications manifest in damaged and poorly functioning organs and organ systems. The complications progress to spiritual hopelessness, helplessness, suicidal tendencies and actual suicide. The social and family conflicts now turn into ruptures, leaving no apparent hope for a social future. And the physical signs and complications become preterminal or terminal. The Romance has run its course and ended in personal disaster.

## Risk Factors

All symptoms, signs and complications are influenced by risk factors. All need to be assessed before a complete and clear-cut diagnosis or treatment plan can be formulated. Diagnosing and staging a disease requires scientific and skillful methods to establish the nature of a sick person's illness. This is done by evaluating the psycho-social-physical history of the disease process occurring in that individual, by observing signs and symptoms, assessing the complications, doing laboratory tests, physical examinations and other indicated procedures to arrive at the proper stage and nature of the person's infirmity.

The value of establishing a diagnosis is to provide a logical basis for treatment and for a forecast of the course of disease. To have a clear-cut diagnosis and outlook based on understanding the stages of an individual's disease is very helpful to the patient, one's colleagues and members of the family.

Using a diagnostic approach based on stages of severity simplifies the development of a logical treatment plan. Knowing what stage the individual has reached when the diagnosis is made has a great deal to do with predicting the final outcome. This approach also makes it easier to determine who is *not* chemically dependent.

Appendicitis and chronic kidney failure are predictable diseases. That is, we can quite accurately predict what will happen if they go unattached and untreated. Chemical dependency also follows a predictable course to the end.

Unless there is clarity regarding the usual history of a disease and the course it takes, it is difficult to devise treatments that will be efficient and likely to have a successful outcome. Unless we know the stage of disease an individual is experiencing, we will tend to overtreat or undertreat. Either extreme can be detrimental and costly.

We need to continually clarify the difference between signs, symptoms, complications, risk factors, precipitating factors and contributing factors in chemical dependency. And we must also remain aware and possess a working knowledge of the usual course of the illness of chemical dependency. The Public Health model and the aforementioned criteria for symptoms and signs and complications are helpful in acquiring that clarity and knowledge.

**Chemical Dependency Symptoms And Signs**

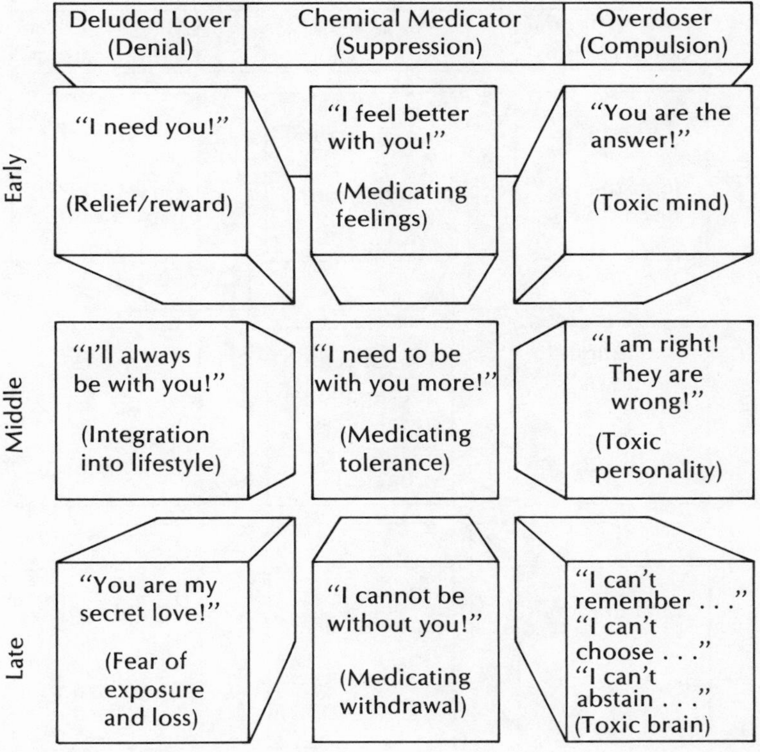


This is a summary of the ***PRIMARY*** disease of chemical dependency, showing the major symptom groups that result from the disease affecting the person's ***BRAIN.***

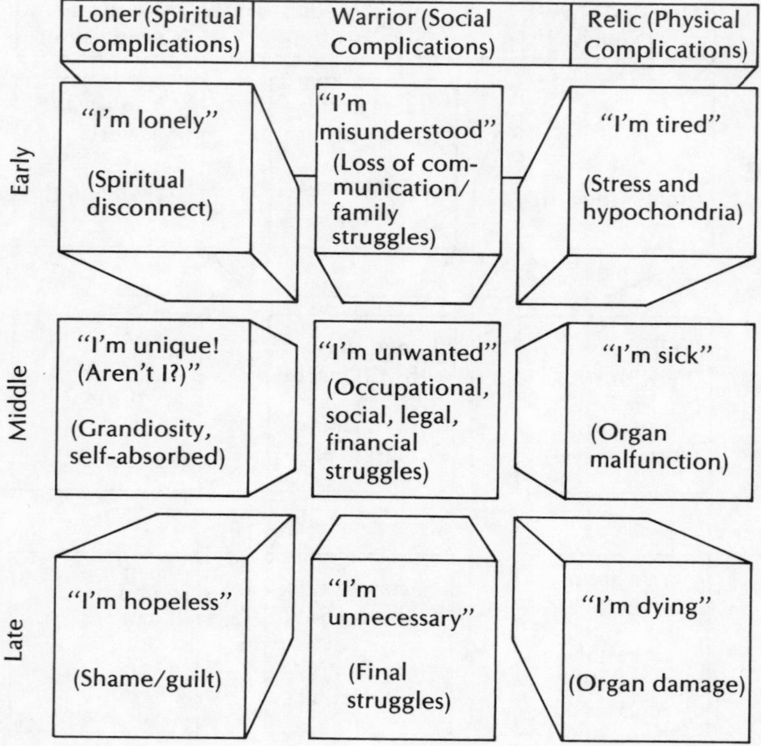


This is a summary of the ***RESULTS*** of having the primary brain disease of chemical dependency which is allowed to progress to secondary complications that affect the patient's ***LIFE.***

# 8

# Target . . . The Brain

When a disease first affects a person's body, it will often seem to affect only one organ or one organ system. Later this disease process may spread throughout the body and cause multiple complications in other organs or organ systems. If left untreated, it can cause death. During its course, any disease that ultimately results in death has great impact on a patient's life. This is especially true with chronic diseases such as arthritis, diabetes or multiple sclerosis. Long before they are fatal, these diseases seriously and agonizingly affect the person's occupational, financial, emotional and spiritual life — and the lives of each person around them, especially the family.

There has been a virtual explosion in recent years of counseling and supportive services, not only for patients with chronic illnesses of many varieties, but also for family members of those patients. Alcoholism is no exception.

A few years ago if a general audience was asked which organ was the primary target of alcoholism, the resounding answer was the liver. This was an error. The target organ of mind- and mood-altering chemicals, such as alcohol and other drugs, is the brain. Now audiences are more sophisticated, and frequently you will hear less of the liver and more of the brain.

Over the last 30 years the general public, along with the scientific and medical communities, have become aware of the importance of the brain in this disease. Early in that period much of the research on the cause of alcoholism centered around the ability of the liver to metabolize alcohol properly. In the meantime the argument on whether alcoholism and drug addiction were truly primary diseases of the human body flared. No logical basis or description of its development was universally accepted. The argument continues today, even though we are learning more and more about brain defects and brain differences in those who suffer from chemical dependency.

It is interesting to note that of 24 articles on alcoholism in a 1981 issue of *The Scientific Journal on Alcoholism* the majority dealt with the effects of alcohol on certain other organs, especially the liver. A symposium, reported in the same journal, on the effects of alcohol on the brain hardly alluded to any possible cause and effect relationship.

This can be compared with a 1987 issue of *The American Journal of Psychiatry*. In that issue, nine out of 13 articles dealt with either the metabolism or anatomy of the brain as a cause for addiction and also as the underlying basis for other mental disorders including schizophrenia, Alzheimer's and depression.

Psychiatric research has for years looked at the *mind* rather than the *brain* in terms of the causes of psychiatric illness including addictions. Now it is becoming more apparent that functional and structural dysfunctions of the brain are probably at the root of not only addictions, but other mental diseases, too.

As Dr. Nancy Andreasen states, "Psychiatry is only beginning to reclaim the brain as its organ. We are fortunate to specialize in the diseases of the most interesting, complex and important organ of the entire body."

Mark Gold, M.D., founder of the 1-800-COCAINE hotline, says, "Psychiatrists are finally getting out of the mind and into the brain in their attempts to understand and treat mental illnesses."

## Poisoning

For a better understanding of the medical or disease aspects of chemical dependency, it would be well to look at alcoholism and other drug addictions in the light of other disease processes for which we have a more sound foundation.

Alcoholism and druggism are problems that involve poisoning the normal functioning of the body. That poisoning, or impairment, is a disease. But since so many people have a problem understanding how addiction can be considered a disease, we are going to explain the disease process in this chapter.

A disease is literally a "lack of ease; a pathological condition of the body that presents a group of symptoms particular to it and which sets the condition apart as an abnormal entity differing from other normal or abnormal body states." (Taber)

In medicine it is usually required that a disease be a true entity, having a specific process that manifests a set of signs and symptoms and has a described course. The argument as to whether alcoholism is a disease has been made more difficult by the disagreements on what is disease and what is health per se. It has been difficult to describe the exact body process that the disease of chemical dependency takes.

Diseases of the human body are classified under four major groups of causes:

1. Congenital diseases are defects present at birth and affecting the structure of the body and its functioning.
2. Metabolic diseases are those in which the body is unable to properly utilize, break down or excrete substances in a normal fashion due to an error in the way the body handles substances or because of the toxicity of the substances.

3. Infectious diseases take over the body in the form of foreign organisms, such as bacteria, parasites or viruses, which disrupt the normal functioning of the body.
4. Traumatic diseases are injuries and accidents that result in the dysfunction of the body.

Knowing these four major categories of disease and dysfunction in the human body, where do we place drug addiction and alcoholism? Evidence is mounting that a difference in the metabolism, or the ability of the body to handle mind- and mood-altering chemicals, results in the full-blown disease of chemical dependency. Therefore, the disease would be classified as metabolic.

## Abnormal Metabolism

Abnormal metabolism also results from taking in noxious substances, such as inhaling lead fumes or asbestos particles. The amount of the toxic agent introduced into the body is of great importance. Human bodies can tolerate trace amounts of strychnine, moderate amounts of alcohol and small amounts of marijuana or cocaine without any noticeable effect. It is where amounts are high enough for a resulting adverse effect that we say there is a person who is toxic, intoxicated, poisoned or overdosed.

The entry of lead into the human body over a long period of time can have fatal effects. Workers and persons who work with stained glass must be careful not to inhale lead fumes. Lead poisoning initially affects the red blood cells and can result in an anemia. Also if the disease goes untreated, it can spread throughout the body and affect a person's emotional and psychological life. Acute lead poisoning is rare. But chronic lead poisoning is sometimes an industrial disease or may occur from drinking water carried in older lead pipes. It is interesting that an overdose of lead or an overdose of alcohol on a regular and recurring basis, or an overdose of cocaine or barbituates, may produce intestinal problems, weakness of muscles, anemia, mental disturbances, loss of appetite, irritability, aggressiveness, sleep disturbance and memory lapses. These are the results of chronic or long-term exposure to toxic doses of a chemical.

But why does alcohol or other mood-altering chemical toxicity result in the individual wanting to go back to become toxic again and again? We do not understand this. However, it may be related to the fact that the brain changes mind- and mood-altering chemicals so an individual has a temporary sense of well-being, a loss of reality and a new but passing sense of self-worth and euphoria. Emotional pain is diminished, if not eradicated, for a time.

Why do some brains continue to search for an addictive approach to spiritual and emotional comfort? We don't know. It may be that there are errors in the metabolism due to a brain's inherited inability to fully metabolize certain compounds in what we would call normal fashion. This inability may be inherited or it may be acquired.

## Kidney Failure And Symptoms Of Alcoholism

We know that when an organ cannot function completely, there is a build up of either secondary metabolites or waste products, which causes major changes in the way a person appears, behaves and feels. This can eventually be fatal.

An example of this would be kidney failure. Early behavioral symptoms of kidney failure include apathy, fatigue, drowsiness, lethargy and social withdrawal. Mood changes may range from emotional numbness to irritability and excitability with demanding behavior and angry outbursts.

Early intellectual effects of kidney failure come and go. They include the inability to concentrate, decreased attention span and impaired recent and long-term memory. Psychological testing often shows a deterioration in nonverbal intelligence. As uremia (kidney failure) progresses, symptoms of anorexia, weight loss and decreased sexual interest may lead to diagnosis of depression. Total or partial impotence is also common in patients with chronic uremia.

The cause, a toxic nervous system regularly inundated with large amounts of unexcreted chemical waste products, is one possible reason.

Notice the striking similarity between the symptoms of kidney failure and the symptoms of alcoholism. Those similarities get the point across that toxic levels of chemicals in the body, as in addiction, result in disease. As with other metabolic diseases, chemical dependency can affect the function of many organs long before actual organ damage occurs.

Kidney disease starts with a specific organ and later affects other organs or organ systems. In diseases such as chemical dependency, damage to other organs can appear quite late in the course of the illness. The disease may be in place, affecting brain functions many years before other obvious organ problems begin to arise.

Usually an individual with chemical dependency is suffering from a cluster of other complications of the illness by the time physical complications appear. Spiritual, legal, social, marital and family life may be disrupted. The person's occupational life may be in jeopardy before physical symptoms appear.

We are not absolutely certain about the nature of the toxic effects of alcohol and other mood-altering chemicals on the brain. But information is rapidly accumulating regarding the manner in which the brain sends messages to itself and to the rest of the body through its "neurotransmitter" system and its myriad of nerve cells and nerve bundles. It seems that the long-term excessive use of mood-altering chemicals causes certain brain centers to lose their ability to function properly. The brain centers for logic, intuition, insight, perception, memory and our belief system are surely affected. Adverse changes in these centers during the time of intoxication carry over to times between bouts of intoxication and can become permanent.

The brain is a particularly difficult organ to study. Therefore, it has become one of the last frontiers for human investigation. The anatomy of the brain has been well-known for years, but how it functions has been relegated mainly to animal studies and electronic mappings and the use of X-ray studies. Now we have new measuring techniques, such as radio-isotopes and imaging scanners, and better animal models to study. So information is beginning to accumulate about this most mysterious and complicated organ.

Richard M. Restak, M.D., in his excellent book *The Brain, The Last Frontier,* says the brain cannot be thought of as just an organ but rather as a process. This process is built on a static fixed anatomy, but that anatomy has no meaning unless we consider its action. Restak likens the process of the mind to the workings of our government. Congress, the White House and the Supreme Court are things. Their workings are the process of government. Our brains, spinal cords and nervous systems are things. Our mind, thoughts and feelings are processes that take place within and around that brain, spinal cord and nervous system.

Richard Bergland, M.D., states we are learning so much about neurotransmitters, using chemicals to send messages, that the brain should probably no longer be considered "dry and electrical but rather wet and hormonal." He then gives evidence for resurrecting the concept that the brain is a *master gland!* If this is true, it will make the job of research and treatment more logical and substantative. Chasing and modifying chemical thoughts and feelings of the brain has more substance to it than chasing and modifying electrical thoughts and feelings.

Once we learn the normal and abnormal chemical pathways that occur in chemical dependency, we should be able to demonstrate to the patient how to adjust, stimulate or suppress those pathways so they can recover from their disease.

**Three Brains**

Paul McClain, M.D., is one of the country's major proponents of the belief that we do not have one brain, but three. He suggests that there is a "reptile brain," which is the primitive brain involved in our physical survival when danger or enemies come near. The reptile brain is where fight or flight without fright occurs. It is the same self-preservation behavior that we see in all animals.

The second brain, which Dr. McClain calls "mammalian," folds around the first brain and is called the cortex. It fills most of the skull and has quite different functions from the reptilian brain. It seems to be involved with our sense of love, caring about community and children, and caring about the ongoing existence of our planet and species. It inculcates sexual love as well as ferocity. This mammalian or midbrain controls and contains much emotional energy. It is the seat of our emotions. One of those emotions is fear. Fear energy can be joined with the reptilian brain to provide a ferocious self-preserving fight to the death.

The third brain of our body is the newest in terms of evolution and only represents a small amount of the cortex covering our entire brain. It is sometimes called the neocortex, meaning new brain. It is an extremely complicated brain and does not seem to be used to its full potential. All brains in the animal world seem to be enlarging from generation to generation. However, the human brain seems to enlarge 20 percent faster than what seems to be necessary. The only other animal with such rapid brain growth is the dolphin.

It has been postulated that intelligent people today use only a hundredth of their neocortex and perhaps geniuses such as Einstein only used a fiftieth of the total available cortex. The brain is apparently organized as the central processing unit for the rest of our nervous system, our hormones, our muscles, tendons, digestive system and so forth.

The poet Robert Bly speaks to the energy distribution in the brain in his book, *Leaping Poetry.* He discusses how poets differ because of different energies sent to the different levels of their brains. He also feels that a separate apportionment is made in each brain, and whichever of our three brains receives the most energy will determine the tone of the individual personality. All of us change and utilize our three different brains constantly.

The brain section that seems to give us most of our sense of well-being is the midbrain or mammalian brain. Most of the neurotransmitters having to do with feelings of wellness, worth and safety reside there. We know that actual chemical changes in this area of the brain result from certain activities, chemicals and medications. Our limbic system can be stimulated to send out chemical signals that "all is well." There are some studies to indicate that jogging and other types of exercise stimulate certain neurotransmitters, giving us a feeling of being "up" or euphoric.

It is probably in these areas of the brain that external mind-altering chemicals, such as alcohol and cocaine, do their work. In the chemically dependent person, the brain incorporates these external chemicals into its own functioning. The chemically dependent brain then comes to a point where it can only function in the presence of the mind-altering chemicals. Or at least it cannot function comfortably and efficiently without them. The presence of these external chemicals literally becomes a way of life for the brain. The taking in of these external chemicals becomes a way of life for the person.

It seems well established now that there is a primary biochemically based disorder in certain individuals which blossoms into a full-blown dependency on mood-altering chemicals. The belief that all chemical dependency is secondary to some other underlying psychological and emotional disorder is no longer tenable. There are many individuals who suffer psychological and emotional disorders and utilize mood-altering chemicals to medicate the pain of their problems. Some of these people become metabolically addicted. Others can take or leave these drugs without serious changes or consequences of any significance.

The vast majority of chemically dependent persons, many of whom may also have emotional and psychological problems, are metabolically programmed to become dependent on these chemicals. As long as they use chemicals, they will continue to suffer the consequences and symptoms of their disease. Even if associated psychological problems clear up or change, they will remain addicted and dependent if they expose themselves to chemicals. Currently, the basic requirement for a return to normalcy by these addicts is total abstinence from mood-altering chemicals.

In summary, since 1976 we have learned that there is a metabolic relationship between alcohol and opiates and the brains of some people that results in a disease called chemical dependency. These chemicals are mainly mood-altering, but also mind-altering. Craving and the constant search for alcohol or other mind-altering chemicals probably result from a deficiency of naturally occurring substances known as neurotransmitters that occur mainly in the brain.

Two of those neurotransmitters that are quite important in the whole schema of addiction are the catacholamines and endorphins, says Dr. Floyd Bloom at the Scripps Institute in La Jolla, California. In many alcoholics genetic differences may cause the abnormality. Other factors may be chronic stress, recurrent stress and long-term compulsive drinking or using. Realizing that functions of the brain are dependent upon chemicals gives us an opportunity to further study, research, treat and perhaps even someday prevent the disease from expression or developing in high risk individuals.

If a condition is to be considered a disease, it has to have a process that can be described and it needs a fairly uniform and unique set of symptoms and signs. Attempts to delineate signs and symptoms and complications in chemical dependency have been extremely confusing and difficult in the past. Most proposed frameworks reflect the profession or background of the designer. The disease of chemical dependency appears differently to a therapist than it does to an emergency room physician, an alcoholism counselor or a long-time Alcoholics Anonymous member.

C. Robert Cloninger, M.D., has described how certain neurotransmitters, the chemicals that come from the brain and send action messages and feeling messages throughout our body, are also involved in the development of our personalities.

## Three Personality Dimensions

Three major dimensions of our personalities have been found to be genetically based. That is, we inherit these personality characteristics through the genes we receive from our parents. Those three personality dimensions are *Novelty-Seeking, Harm-Avoidance* and *Reward Dependence.* Each of these genetically determined dimensions of our personalities are different in varying amounts within each individual. All of us demonstrate some degree of those three dimensions. Under different circumstances and environmental conditions a certain dimension may become predominant. Under other conditions a combination of one, two or three of the dimensions may be predominant. There are systems within the brain that use these genetically-determined dimensions. The Novelty-Seeking dimension uses the *behavioral activation system* of the brain, the Harm-Avoidance dimension uses a *behavioral inhibition system* and the Reward Dependent dimension attempts to maintain the status quo using the *behavioral maintenance system.*

Certain stimuli set off certain individual systems or combinations of systems. For example, the behavioral activation system (Novelty-Seeking) is stimulated into life by the opportunity for novelty or rewards or also by the need for relief from boredom or punishment. The neurotransmitter involved with this system is dopamine. The response we all observe from a person whose behavioral activation system has been stimulated is that of being exploratory and needy. They frequently have and search for constant intense exhilaration. Alcohol stimulates the expression or learned response of the behavioral activation system and novelty-seeking.

The behavioral inhibition system (Harm-Avoidance) is stimulated by the need for relief from punishment, the need to avoid risk-taking and the need to refrain from excess novelty and stimulation and anxiety. The need for relief from frustration and disappointment or potential disappointment also activates this system. The neurotransmitter involved in the behavioral inhibition system is serotonin and some of the stress hormones such as adrenaline and cortisone are involved as well. Someone who has activated his harm-avoidance behavioral inhibition system appears to us as passive, inhibited, probably depressed, withdrawn, reserved and avoiding excess boisterous activity. The basic feeling of a person whose behavioral inhibition system is turned on is that of uniqueness and loneliness. Alcohol blocks the expression of the inhibition system. The person breaks out of their inhibitions under the influence of alcohol, at least initially. Those who use this dimension of harm-avoidance excessively are also at risk for accelerating the use of and dependence on alcohol and other mind/mood-altering chemicals in order to circumvent the consequences of continuous use of avoidant behavior.

The behavioral maintenance system (Reward-Dependence) is stimulated into being by the need for social approval, relief of punishment or continuing of a short-lived exhilaration, secondary to accomplishment. This is medicated through a neurotransmitter called epinephrine and perhaps norepinephrine. These are constantly vigilant in keeping one "ready." Such people appear rigid, persistent, deluded, compulsive and frequently obsessed. Their major feeling is that of being misunderstood, perplexed, and even angry. This system may, though epinephrine, be the basis for tolerance to the sedating effects of alcohol. Therefore, it allows an individual to become seriously intoxicated and lose control. Metabolic tolerance is the resistance to the sedating effect of alcohol or other sedative/hypnotic drugs.

In the novelty-seeking individual, on the other hand, behavioral tolerance occurs. What this then requires is that a behavior that originally brought exhilaration has to be repeated more often, more intensely or in a more increased variety of ways to have the same exhilarating effect.

## Type One And Type Two Alcoholics

Dr. Cloninger breaks alcoholics into two types. He points out that many alcoholics and alcohol abusers have some features of each type. It should be kept clear that the two types are what he calls the "polar extremes of personality traits and that these extremes vary continuously."

***The Type One*** alcoholic demonstrates loss of control and has associated characteristics of those who are passive, dependent or excessively anxious. These persons depend a great deal on rewards; they are eager to help others; they are very sympathetic, sentimental and persistent. In addition to the Reward-Dependent personality dimension, Type One alcoholics also demonstrate high harm avoidance. They are extremely cautious, inhibited, apprehensive and shy. Their Novelty-Seeking dimension is quite low, resulting in becoming rigid, reflective, orderly and compulsive in attention to details. This type of alcoholic is the one who demonstrates loss of control once they begin to drink, even though they can go for long periods without drinking. Women frequently fall into this class.

***Type Two*** alcoholic Dr. Cloninger describes as associated with the triad of characteristics that have an anti-social or borderline personality disorder. It is almost the reverse of the traits seen in the Type One passive-dependent individual. High novelty-seeking, impulsive and exploratory behavior, being excitable and distractable describe the novelty-seeking dimension of the personality. However, associated with that is low harm-avoidance. They are optimistic and uninhibited, they seem to have energy and a somewhat "who cares?" attitude toward risk. They also show low reward-dependence. They do not need social approval. They are detached, cool, tough-minded and frequently seen as independent.

Novelty-seeking, harm-avoidance and reward-dependence can actually be measured. These vary independently one from the other and apparently are genetically inherited, one from the other. Therefore, alcoholics of a pure Type One or pure Type Two would be quite rare, but rather there are variable patterns to "seek out alcohol and to become tolerant to and dependent on it."

Dr. Cloninger goes on to describe other characteristics of the two types of alcoholism. Type One usually occurs after age 25. Fighting and arrests are rare, psychological dependence is frequent and guilt and fear about that dependence is frequent. Type Two alcoholics frequently have their onset before age 25. They have an inability to abstain at all but can perhaps better control their drinking once it has begun, fighting and anti-social behavior are frequent, psychological dependence or loss of control of their drinking is infrequent and they have little guilt or fear about their use or dependence on alcohol.

Other mind- or mood-altering drugs have not been researched nearly as extensively as alcohol, but it is thought that those drugs belonging to the same sedative hypnotic class as alcohol will probably demonstrate similar characteristics of the personality. Such drugs are the barbiturates, tranquilizers and other sleeping and sedative type medications.

As we learn more about the effects on the brain of chemicals, such as alcohol, we become more accepting of addiction as a disease. Knowing the impact chemicals can have on the brain helps us to understand even the denial and delusion that are as much a part of addiction as are its physical manifestations.

PART II

# Co-dependency

# INTRODUCTION

Many professionals, family members and employers feel that once the alcoholic/addict is on a path to recovery and those around them understand that addiction is a disease, the previous difficulties with which they all struggled will be automatically and forever resolved. Many family members hold to the belief and the constant goal that once sobriety is attained, "We can live happily ever after."

The person who is chemically dependent is center stage and the center of attention, especially during using and drinking times. When people recover from their addictions, they are *still* center stage and the center of attention. They are now *finally* a recovering (let's hope he doesn't slip) person!

When spouses of addicts and alcoholics are *treated* at many treatment centers, they learn the basis for the disease of chemical dependency and some of the reasons why they have gone through what they have gone through. They receive assurances that once the addiction is under control, their lives will be under control. Their emotions are described as perfectly natural reactions to an active addiction in the home. They receive little attention to how they are feeling or how inadequately they have been prepared to *do life* while growing up in an alcoholic home.

Individuals suffering from the pain of a family member's addiction have always been there, regardless of age. Some of them are children . . . frozen children . . . lonely children . . . inept children . . . still waiting for help. They all come from dysfunctional families, many from dysfunctional chemically dependent families. They need a special type of help that's more than just learning and knowing.

Treatment providers are beginning to treat family members and others who are close to a using addict/alcoholic. They diagnose these individuals as having their own disease, which is commonly termed *co-dependency.* Some of these programs have three to six months waiting lists for admission. Other alcohol and drug treatment providers continue the traditional mode of the past. They educate the family members regarding alcohol and drugs and disallow the use of co-dependency as a diagnostic term for the family members by their therapeutic staff.

Both the chemically dependent person and the spouse can return home from these treatment centers to their own support groups, such as Alcoholics Anonymous, Narcotics Anonymous, Al-Anon and Naranon. Alateen, a support group for children from alcoholic families, has an off-and-on, somewhat stormy course and has not been completely available throughout the country. Even where it has been offered, children have still stood back. Into their adulthood, after they have left home and are into middle-age, they are still standing back. While they wave their hands politely, attempting to get our attention, they are asking quietly . . . "What about us? . . . What about me? . . ."

In recent years, however, this question has become louder. In a collective way, adult children have begun to fight back. They are changing the course of their own lives and are seeking help. They have made a decision not to wait for the world to change but to change their world. The long-kept secrets about alcoholism or drug addiction in the home have moved outside the home, and clusters of support have developed across the country.

It's not a totally popular happening. As a country, we have made significant social and medical headway in addressing the needs of chemically dependent individuals. The children telling the whole and more complete story are reminders that everyone involved has not been recovering from the disease of co-dependency and chemical dependency as completely as we would like to believe. Recovering addicts and alcoholics who have striven vigorously to overcome their addictions and are glad that the addiction is controlled and that everyone's "troubles are over," are still operating under myths.

There are recovering alcoholics who would prefer that the children and the adult children keep quiet. This message of "keeping quiet" is an old familiar mixed family message and one that children from alcoholic and chemically dependent families know well. "Live in our reality — not yours." Initially, and true to their upbringing, each small cluster of whispering children naturally begins to self-doubt and retreat. Yet larger clusters and larger networks continue to grow. The loud whispers continue, and people are finding each other. Counseling groups and 12-Step self-help groups are proving beneficial to them.

Now there is a groundswell of individuals from alcoholic families demanding help. Many adults, children and adult children, sick and tired of their own pain and their continuing struggle, expect now to recover from their emotional dependencies every bit as much as the chemically dependent persons expect to recover from their drug and alcohol dependencies.

Where are these people coming from? They seem to have swarmed out of the woodwork. They have their own self-help support meetings now. They have their own national office and their own national convention. They have their own list of characteristics for their disease and have their own list of promises for recovery.

Many of them are people who are accustomed to going to self-help meetings, who are comfortable sharing feelings with others and using a 12-Step recovery program. Half of them are recovering from their own dependency. And one of the most exciting and emotionally positive healing events occurring to them is that, like those few recovering alcoholics 50 years ago who founded Alcoholics Anonymous, co-dependents have found each other. Like the spouses of recovering alcoholics 50 years ago, who had their own needs, they recognized the need in each other and have begun to help each other.

Additional advances are being made. Recognition, sharing and connections are leading to a cultural awakening. People working with children from alcoholic families have faced resistance along the way, but they have kept going. They have studied, they have noticed and they have taken and prepared notes. Their writings have appeared and conferences have been held. Adult children, totally isolated for most of their lives, have found others of their own kind. The professionals who have been trying to help them are finding others of their own kind. The groundswell continues today.

# 9

# Co-dependency — Its Origins

Statistics tell us that one in eight American children have a parent with past or present alcoholism and/or drug abuse or addiction. These children suffer mental health problems and personality disorders. Their homes are a source of a high level of chronic stress to them, and they themselves have a high risk of addiction.

An estimated 28.6 million Americans are growing up or have grown up as offspring of alcoholic parents. Nearly seven million of these children are still under the age of 18. We know that only 10-15 percent of active alcoholics and other chemically dependent individuals are receiving treatment themselves. This is partly because of the difficulty in breaking through denial and partly due to enabling "gate-keepers," such as physicians, counselors, law enforcement officials, clergy and educators, who are still not tuned into the prevalence and pervasiveness of the disease of chemical dependency and its partner, co-dependency. These gate-keepers are still not aware that chemical and co-dependency are illnesses of families, in which all members need and will benefit from help of some form or another.

Dr. Ian McDonald, M.D., and Sheila Bloom, M.D., wrote in the *American Journal of Disease of Children* in August of 1987, that two major blocks prevented families of alcoholics and addicts from receiving help sooner. One was the lack of attention to this problem by practicing physicians. They state, "When physicians ask questions in ways that indicate they don't want to know the answer, they don't get the answer." They must know what they are looking for and probe to get it. Unless the physician can demonstrate a persistent, but nonjudgmental attitude and a general feeling of hopefulness, ". . . only the most blatant, chronic and last-stage cases will be detected."

Many authorities have stated that the misconceptions about the disease of alcoholism and other chemical dependencies block families from getting help. The major misconceptions are . . .

- That the attainment of abstinence by the parent will reverse the family's problems.
- That nothing can be done to help the child as long as the parent continues to drink.

## Adult Children Of Alcoholics

Children do recover from co-dependency, much of the time outside their family. They are recovering in greater numbers now because of the numerous adult children of alcoholic treatment programs that are available and because of the ever-expanding movement of adult children of alcoholics self-help groups. When a person does recover from co-dependency, they frequently wake up to the fact that others in the family are still swimming in pathology. This makes their own recovery even more difficult, because they are now the one who is looked upon as being "different." They become the "scapegoat," the "rebel," the "odd one."

The most obvious examples of co-dependents are persons from alcoholic families, and children are the best examples of those persons, especially when they have become adults and continue to carry the pathology.

Why is this important? It is important because of the myth that co-dependency is simply a painful adult reaction to growing up in an alcoholic home. When the active addiction ceases, does the painful reaction cease? No.

The concept of co-dependency is important because of the high incidence of chemical dependency among children from alcoholic families. It's important because of the high incidence of marriage and remarriage of alcoholics to alcoholics and co-dependents to alcoholics. It is important because in the average family of four where there is a chemically dependent person, there are four times the number of co-dependents (including the chemically dependent) who need help. Recovery from both is a must for such a family. Recovery from either one is incomplete recovery.

Recovery from co-dependency is important because the active co-dependent suffers from insecurity, lack of trust, unresolved anger and guilt, and difficulty in establishing a career path or any kind of adult intimate relationship. Unattended co-dependency eliminates the greatest part of good living for a great number of individuals. Unresolved co-dependency affects the workplace. These people become less productive, less cooperative, less innovative as time goes on.

## The Dysfunctional Home

People coming from an alcoholic or otherwise dysfunctional home are stunted in their emotional growth. At some point in their development, their growth ceases. Perhaps this happened at a very young age when they were toddlers and pre-school children. To them it seems as if "my child died inside of me." These individuals then pass into adulthood and physical maturity without the emotional growth and maturity needed to accompany it. Though their actions, beliefs, concepts and behaviors are modified and redecorated so as to appear appropriate in adulthood, the basic underlying drives and reactions remain emotionally childish or adolescent.

Children from dysfunctional homes do not recover as they enter the adult world. They remain separated from their realities (feelings). When it comes time for them to marry, they often marry into pathology. They look for someone who appears normal to them, as they have learned to perceive normal. Reality is not one of the child's strong suits. As the parents have gone through their periods of disenchantment, and as chemical dependency in one of the parents has begun to flare into its middle and late stages, children do not just stand by as innocent observers or simple reactors. They begin their own pathological thinking, feeling and behavior patterns.

Attempting to learn healthy coping skills from dysfunctional parents is impossible. Children watch the co-dependent parent go through feelings of embarrassment, humiliation and anger and then stuff those feelings. Children are experts at recognizing role plays, myths and games, and frequently see the spouse of the alcoholic displaying false hope and encouragement. The children learn to predict disappointment, hurt, confusion and chaos. They also become expert at stuffing feelings. They watch as social isolation and distrust become the norm for the family and believe that social isolation and distrust must be normal throughout the world.

## Family Focus

Drinking or using may become the focus within that family. The drinker or the user becomes blaming and shaming of the spouse, and the spouse becomes blaming and shaming of the drinker or user. And each child becomes blamed and shamed in its own mind. The child, who at one time as "king baby" of the family saw itself as responsible for everything in its world as it lay in its crib, now has in some way or other caused laughter and joy to become sadness and pain. The child watches as loss of communication and episodes of failure are followed by false hope and temporary gain and then again disaster. The child watches as control over others seems to work for a while and then anger, anxiety, silence or nagging are needed as a temporary means of coping.

The child might not identify such events as a problem with chemicals or alcohol at all, but rather as a problem of ordinary living and being — the stuff that life is made of. Chaos becomes normal. Guilt, shame and loss of self-respect and self-confidence begin to eat away at the spiritual foundation of the child. Self-worth begins to plummet.

At some point self-indulgence and self-comfort, accompanied by self-neglect or self-abuse, begin to occur. Children begin to have thoughts about chemicals which they have seen can at least bring temporary relief. Children begin to experiment and experience actual relief from using chemicals or from controlling others. They may learn the relief of isolating themselves. They develop their own perception of a reality that is, in and of itself, a myth. Each child says to herself or himself, "This is the real life." And the brain tucks that away. Then the challenge for the child is to design, create and conduct a workable fantasy life, regardless of the sensations, impulses, information, emotions and knowledge that are pouring reality into the brain.

## Denial Of The Emotions

Many children from alcoholic families believe they are in situations that they cannot change. They may even go so far as to believe the situation does not need changing. They use their brain to go into their own state of denial. The denial becomes so great that they can normalize anything that is happening in their chaotic, abusive lives. They quickly begin to suppress any painful emotions. If the emotions cannot be suppressed, then they project them onto others or transform them. And if the painful emotions cannot be projected or transformed, they are tolerated in silence for that is the proper way to do it. The children suffer without a sound.

Persons who learn a lifestyle of denial say such things as, "It isn't so bad," or, "It wasn't so bad." They can die or wither on the vine from that much denial.

A dysfunctional family can abuse children even though there may not be physical abuse. Emotional abuse, lack of affirmation, lack of physical contact or lack of caring for physical needs are all forms of abuse. Children from chemically dependent families can carry their denial so far that they rarely blame the parents or the drinking or drugging in the family. They blame themselves. They believe that no other family is quite like theirs, and that it would be different (better) if they weren't in it or if they knew how to act as a member of it. They pretend that everything is okay. They behave with a secret agenda to gain their goal for the day, just as a chemically dependent person does so they won't be found out. They keep secret their means of coping, their "medicating" behavior, their embarrassment, their loneliness and their pain.

As youngsters dependent for their physical needs on others who happen to be adults, they cannot obey their inner messages to "fight or flee." They also cannot connect, love, feel loved or even give love, so they rearrange their reality in spite of their feelings. To keep those feelings swallowed requires ongoing suppressive behavior and energy, perhaps medication by chemicals, or perhaps both. And indeed many children from alcoholic families end up chemically dependent as well.

## Compulsive Behavior

Those who do not find relief in chemicals learn to use compulsive types of behavior, such as overeating or gambling, to control and separate their feelings from themselves. However, when we separate our feelings from ourselves, we separate ourselves from reality. Our feelings were given to each of us to help measure and evaluate our inside and our outside worlds. Without them, we are in much less reality, even in a void.

In 1958, Bill Wilson, one of the founders of Alcoholics Anonymous, stated in an article entitled, "Love," that, ". . . when we are completely and emotionally dependent on someone else, *we must control them.*" That need to control comes from the fear that the other person will walk away, leaving us to fall flat on our face, leaving us alone in the world. Our self-worth is tied up in our relationship with that person, leaving us worth less and ultimately worthless. We must control in order to stay attached. Children in alcoholic families become more and more sophisticated in their ability to control, repress and deny. However, their faces and bodies begin to show that effort even at an early age. Just as the alcoholic/addict becomes a young relic, so does the co-dependent.

Some of the means co-dependents use to suppress and avoid confronting emotional pain are the medicating behaviors we have mentioned. These give some relief, which is short-lived. Medicating behaviors, therefore, are used as drugs. They need to be repeated frequently and with more vigor each time to be of any benefit. After a while, they need to be combined with other medicating behaviors to attain any result whatsoever, just as it is in the case of alcohol and drugs and prescription pills for some addicts.

Some behaviors are "busy-ness," "busybody" activity and workaholism. We know the temporary relief from being a human who is "doing things," rather than a person who is just "being" when that "being" is in pain. Food is a medicator. The control over food and therefore the control over people as well — combined with a preoccupation with body image — can result in obesity, anorexia or the rush that comes from the purging of food (bulimia). The rush and temporary relief comes through the actual release of serotonin, a brain chemical with feeling-good look-alike effects. Other medicators may be nonintimate compulsive sexual acting out and using one's own sexuality in a manner that can be termed sexuality abuse. Gambling and the "green-paper pathology" of spending, buying, repeated owning and investing all serve as temporary medicators.

Increased doses of alcohol or drugs increase brain dysfunctions and affect and threaten a person's life. The activities and behavior of a co-dependent can also result in physical, spiritual and social disruptions that can end fatally. *More* becomes the order of the day. More work, more accomplishments, more material things, more power, more "love," more cigarettes, more food, more sex, more, more, more.

With a new behavior, an individual's urgings, cravings and fears are quieted — just for the moment. In order to maintain relief it becomes necessary to increase frequency, intensity, duration and manners of behaving.

When such co-dependent behaviors begin to appear abnormal to the outside world, the co-dependent person goes underground to prevent discovery or interruption. The major question for them, just as for the alcoholic Lover, is, "How can I continue to satisfy my cravings, calm my fears and slow my urgings and not get found out?" These are the same questions that an addict and an alcoholic ask about the use of their drug, "How can I get at it, get it down and get rid of the evidence?"

## Co-dependency Sufferers

Those who are most likely to suffer from the disease of co-dependency are children and spouses from chemically dependent families. We can also include children and spouses from other types of dysfunctional families. The adult children from these dysfunctional families, who have missed the needed help over their first 20 to 30 years, also continue to suffer from the dysfunctions.

Grandchildren and siblings of chemically dependent persons can also show the effects of this disease. A grandchild may have two abstaining parents who themselves never succumb to chemical dependency, but their co-dependency disease was already in place and went untreated. The grandchild can suffer from being raised by these untreated parents. The behaviors, traits and perhaps even genetics of one or both diseases can be passed on.

Chemically dependent persons, who frequently come from a background of co-dependency and a high incidence of chemical dependency, are themselves co-dependent. Therefore, special treatment and recovery issues that revolve around the recovery program of a chemically dependent person must take into account their co-dependency issues as well. Ignoring co-dependency issues can undermine the chances for recovery from chemical dependency. The "dry drunk syndrome" and relapse appear to be untreated or incompletely treated co-dependency.

Children from painful or emotionally suppressed families, who have rigid rules and allow no questioning about events or questioning of authority figures, frequently suffer from the disease of co-dependency. They learn early on that there is to be no expressing feelings or complaining. They also learn there are no boundaries in this family and there is little recognition of individuals *per se.* There is little guaranteed accountability as well in such a family.

Children assume and want to continue to believe that the family is trustworthy and dependable and can be counted on to be there for them. This includes Mom and Dad and sister and brother and even the family cat. In healthy families this does hold true. In painful suppressed families this truth does not exist.

Individual family members have been hurting silently for years, long after the recovery from chemical addiction has taken place in one of their family members. They learned early on not to complain, not to feel, not to tell anyone, not to trust.

## Signs And Symptoms Of Co-dependency

Since co-dependency is a disease of silence, it is especially valuable for physicians, therapists and other helping professionals to have a framework for identifying it. Perhaps it would be helpful to take a look at the mechanisms by which co-dependency can develop. What are the signs and symptoms that can occur within an individual to such a degree as to cause disruption and dysfunction? Perhaps if we can study and separate the signs and symptoms of co-dependency *within* the person's brain (as we did in chemical dependency), then accurately and clearly separate the complications that occur in a co-dependent's *life* (as we did for the disease of chemical dependency), these questions can be better answered.

Many of the symptoms and signs seen in alcoholics or addicts are also present in non-using family members and in the family as a unit. Family members suffer from a denial that is anything but normal. Expectations and rules, both implicit and explicit, are silently founded within the family and carry a great deal of power in determining the behavior and reactions of its members. Due to minimizing, the true pathology within the family goes undetected.

When there is a single active focus of attention by the entire family, individual needs go unattended. The children suffer because of poor communication and may actually be victimized by a permissiveness that gives them no guidelines for living whatsoever. Undersocialization, neglect, violence, inattention and unrest are standard in such a family. Early minimization of events surrounding drinking and using later turn into maximizing delusion, in which children construct or invent stories, patterns of behavior and scripts of dialogue to explain the paradoxical, painful life they are leading.

One-way communication may occur between the addict and the spouse. The children are expected to listen but not be heard, not question nor react, not acknowledge reality. As the disease progresses, prolonged absences of one or both parents, intimidation, separation, sexual weaponry, emotional deprivation, increasing fear and fear of abandonment occur. Arguments and threats are overheard and thought of as final, time and time again. Each time is more fearful and final than the last. What does a kid know? The family suffers from neglect, anarchy, chaos, no communication, frequent desertion and violence that is either threatened or actual. Infidelity in a nonsexual marriage results. Separations and divorces are necessary.

Where does this leave the children? Well, as families are the nucleus of our society, so are the children the nucleus of the family. And they know it:

> They start out as "king baby." They rule their roost. They do not question their power. It's there from the beginning. They confirm their power repetitively every day as infants. They are center stage in the morning. They are center stage all day, and they are certainly center stage at bedtime. They have little doubt that this man and this woman are together for the sole purpose of raising them. With this in mind, little wonder that they take credit and feel responsible for happy times . . . and little wonder (as we adults are always surprised to find out) that they also take full responsibility and feel blame, shame and guilt for all of the sad times and troubles that may beset a family.

These little adults don't question it or voice it . . . and we don't know how to inform them of their error. This error is then carried by them, if not all through their life, frequently well into adulthood. Hopefully, they find knowledge, enlightenment and guidance in an active recovery program of their own.

If someone is an addict or an alcoholic, they are also co-dependent. When a chemically dependent co-dependent ignores their co-dependency, there is a greater chance for a relapse, for a "dry drunk," for acting out, for possible burnout. An alcoholic or addict's co-existing primary disorder of co-dependency must not be left untreated. Sadly, it often is left out and a "sad sobriety" or "raging sobriety" is the result.

## Toxic Co-dependency

In Part I the applicability of a Public Health Model (a toxic agent, a susceptible person and a permissive environment) to chemical dependency was discussed.

Does this model also fit for co-dependency? It does with the following considerations. That is, that the toxic agent exists in the brain as a consuming obsession with a belief or a concept. It appears outwardly in the form of repetitive and/or compulsive behavior. True self-worth is lost when a person decides that their own perceived self-worth depends totally on a dedicated and cemented relationship with an individual, a behavior, a belief or an institution. Our perceptions, behaviors and dependencies on others for our self-worth become toxic agents to our brains, sometimes more efficient and more powerful than many chemicals.

When a "toxin" in a person's life is an individual who is chemically addicted and seriously co-dependent, then the stage is set for bilateral or two-way dysfunction.

A person becomes completely dependent on a toxin by enmeshment with it. An institution or philosophy or even a political party can be such a "toxin." A demanding university or corporation, which gives individuals their self-worth and their reason for being, will experience a lot of mid-life career crises, a lot of frustration and passive/aggressive behavior from employees whose early track record was admirable. "Toxic" agents do indeed exist in various forms.

As we stated before, susceptible persons are those who have been raised in alcoholic or chemically dependent homes, where there has been physical and emotional abuse, or in homes where there has been other types of dysfunction. While growing up in these dysfunctional homes, individuals learn that certain behaviors (toxins) give them at least temporary respite from emotional pain. These behaviors, carried into adulthood, frequently no longer work. Yet because of their past history of success, the susceptible person uses them and vigorously adheres to them even after the environment and society says, "No more!"

The beliefs that exist in alcoholic homes, mostly based on myths and perceptions of what works and what really is, remain steadfast in a person's memory. They are used as a basis and a cause for later toxic behavior. Early and complete release of such beliefs is needed to initiate the healing process, but the allegiance to these beliefs is so great that it often prevents recovery from ever occurring.

One subtle basis for this allegiance to toxic and self-defeating behavior is that certain compulsive and repetitive behaviors that worked in childhood also work in adulthood and in fact, are laudatory in our society. The environment is most permissive. Workaholism, detail compulsiveness, controlling and caring for others and people-pleasing are frequently rewarded in our society. Becoming a "company man," instead of your own man, or becoming a completely sacrificing and doting mother, rather than your own woman, is frequently set as a goal for many young men and women as they grow up. Initially, these individuals appear strong; soon they become susceptible.

With "toxic" behaviors and beliefs existing in susceptible persons, allowed and encouraged by a permissive environment, we can divide the disease of co-dependency into a clearer description based on the same framework we used for chemical dependency.

The signs and symptoms of co-dependency result from the direct effects of "toxic" behaviors, individuals and institutions on a susceptible person's *brain.* The complications of co-dependency arise from the direct effects of "toxic" behaviors, individuals and institutions on the person's *life.*

Now that we have seen how co-dependency develops and described its major symptoms and signs, have we clearly established that it is indeed a disease? There are still differing viewpoints on this issue.

## What Is Co-dependency?

***Sondra Smalley,*** Director of Dependencies Institute of Minnesota, sees co-dependency as . . .

> ". . . A term used to describe an exaggerated dependent pattern of learned behaviors, beliefs and feelings that make life painful. It is the dependence on people and things outside of self, along with the neglect of self, to the point of having little self-identity."

Smalley, however, has been quoted as saying that co-dependency is not an actual illness and that the individual must "scourge the disease, the cancer, if you will." Pattern is a word that she uses, emphasizing that co-dependency is a learned coping mechanism that can affect all types of personalities.

***Robert Subby,*** Director of Family Systems, Inc., Minneapolis, describes co-dependency as . . .

> ". . . An emotional psychological behavioral condition that develops as a result of the individual's prolonged exposure to and practice of a set of oppressive rules — rules that prevent the open expression of feeling, as well as the discussion of personal and interpersonal problems."

However, Subby also stays away from any medical basis for the disease, preferring that it be based on a pattern of incomplete development. He especially emphasizes that there are missed stages of childhood and, therefore, identity development difficulties.

For instance, the child doesn't learn the difference between trust and mistrust or autonomy versus dependency because co-dependents are forced to mature at an early age, at least on the surface. They haven't completed their developmental tasks and actually lack a sense of their own being. Subby has suggested that co-dependency be classified in its own diagnostic category called "Delayed Identity Development Syndrome."

***Sharon Wegscheider-Cruse*** has defined co-dependency as . . .

> ". . . A specific condition that is characterized by preoccupation and extreme dependence (emotional, social and sometimes physical) on a person, on a concept or belief, on an object or an institution. Eventually this dependence on something outside oneself becomes a pathological condition that affects the co-dependent in all other relationships."

Wegscheider-Cruse is indicating that there are indeed patterns or traits of behavior, but that when the traits or patterns are carried to extremes or chronic excesses, they then become a pathological condition. In essence, they become a disease. Pathology connotes disease.

***Dr. Timmen L. Cermak*** says . . .

> ". . . Co-dependency represents a fascinating effort to understand a type of dysfunctional human behavior which is disturbingly prevalent. There has been no generally accepted definition for co-dependency."

He states further that most descriptions of co-dependency have been anecdotal or metaphoric and that neither anecdotal nor metaphoric descriptions stand up well under scientific scrutiny.

So when we talk about the behaviors of those who are from families with addiction or other types of dysfunction, are we talking about just simply their behaviors and reactions? Or are we talking about a specific pathology that develops within them? Probably the answer boils down to what many issues boil down to . . . a matter of degree of severity . . . whether a condition is spiritually, socially or physically life-threatening to the degree that it can be identified and classified as a disease.

Dr. Cermak proceeds to attempt to define co-dependency at a level of sophistication equal to the standards set forth in the national Diagnostic and Statistical Manual of the American Psychiatric Association. He uses the definitions of traits versus disorders from the manual to clarify why definitions of co-dependency vary so widely.

According to the manual, personality traits are "enduring patterns of perceiving, relating to and thinking about the environment and one's self." Personality traits only become disorders (or diseases) when they are "inflexible and maladaptive and cause either significant impairment in social or occupational functioning or significant subjective distress." (DSM-IIIR).

## Personality Traits

It could be added that traits become disorders when they cause actual physical distress as well. Medicine now recognizes that emotional states affect physical well-being. We are quite aware of the impact of different personality types (Type A, Type B) on physical well-being, the development of disease or the recovery from an illness. It appears on the surface as though almost everyone suffers from co-dependency when the symptoms are listed and analyzed. But, as Dr. Cermak says, the critical point is that while co-dependent traits may be widespread and pervasive, diagnosis of a co-dependent personality disorder can only be made "when identifiable dysfunction results from obsessive rigidity or intensity that is associated with these traits."

This sounds familiar if the terms obsessive rigidity or intensity are synonyms for severity.

For example, the severity of joint pain may be of no significance or it may be strong enough or constant enough to indicate the disease of arthritis. Likewise, the severity of a paralyzing dependence of one person upon the affections and opinions of another certainly would indicate a diseased state called co-dependency. When a well-defined process of disruption of the normal steady state of psychological and/or physiological functioning is present we have a disease (Gonella). How such a process originates or develops does not change the fact that it is a disease.

So when the "patterns" described by Subby and Smalley become well-defined models of increasingly severe disruptions of the normal steady state in an individual's psychological and physiological functioning, we do then indeed have a disease.

Other authors have wrestled with this entire concept all the way from the specific disorder of *co-addiction,* with its specific set of diagnostic criteria, as described by Dr. James Cocores. Dr. Cocores' criteria almost entirely focus on the reactions of family members to a drinking member. They do not include the more general dysfunctional signs and symptoms that Dr. Cermak's criteria do.

At the other end of the spectrum are those authors who wrestle with the idea that becoming too specific might bypass and ignore some of the more generalized needs of such patients. Therefore, they feel that co-dependency should continue to be viewed as a ". . . general and pervasive dynamic of the painful side of the human condition" (Whitfield). Whitfield fears that if co-dependency is considered a very distinct disorder, there would be the potential that health care providers would attend to just that specific area alone and neglect or miss other important treatable general conditions in their patients.

In spite of this concern, it is believed that the benefits of using a specific disease model to describe co-dependency far outweigh any potential drawbacks. The importance of defining a disease is that we then must come up with a defined treatment for that disease. In treating a specific and well-defined disorder, treatment becomes specific and well-defined. Both patient and therapist are synchronized. The disease has a better outlook, has a sound basis and progress in recovery can be more accurately measured.

A general disorder treated in a general manner, while ignoring *multiple* specific needs, can result in a hit-or-miss partial recovery. Some needs are met *(hit)* while others are not met *(miss)*. Repetitive and prolonged treatment experiences are seen with general treatment approaches. The individual is always working *on* everything while never working *through* any one thing.

Specificity does not mean narrow focus. Specificity allows for more sophisticated treatment and probably a more favorable outcome. However, the holistic or general approach must also be used to aid us in identifying the other dire needs of the patient. Both approaches are in order and actually are not in opposition to one another.

In summary, human conditions and human states exaggerated into disorders become generalized and pervasive, but they also have specific disease subsets which require attention and well-considered treatment interventions and techniques.

# 10

# Control By Denial (Thinking)

## The Deluded Lover

Although its fine structure is very complicated, the development of co-dependency breaks into basically three major symptom groups. The three large symptom groups described by Sharon Wegscheider-Cruse are Compulsive Behavior, Repression of Feelings and Denial of Reality. Actually they represent the same groupings that we described earlier. Having needs *(I need it);* meeting those needs *(I'll try it)* and being reinforced by learning how to meet those needs and integrating that into part of one's brain *(I found it).* As the medicating behavior is repeated over and over, it becomes a total and complete part of our lifestyle with no amendments, moderation, innovation, modification or selection. It becomes a compulsive, choiceless and life-threatening behavior.

## I Need It

Deluded Lovers are initially obsessed and compulsive in their behavior toward each other and toward the relationship, just as addicts are toward their chemical. Co-dependents have needs, such as acceptance, validation and approval, which they have not learned how to have met in healthy ways. They become obsessed with meeting those needs, sending unknowingly desperate emotional signals. Their trial-and-error and experimentation courtship is successful in finding means of coping and medicating. They become infatuated with whatever medicating behavior works the first time, believing it will always work. The infatuation blossoms into a full-blown romance and they struggle through an illicit affair. It appears this way . . .

1. As infants we all go through the stage of not knowing we are separate from our parents and the world around us. When we do learn we are separate beings, we have a heady sense of our power as "king baby," able to control our surroundings. Co-dependents growing up in families where their sense of validation or self-worth comes only from outside circumstances or other people, do not grow beyond this "king baby" stage. They learn that controlling their environment and people around them gives them a "high" or a "rush." They begin an affair with control, just as the addict begins an affair with a chemical.
2. The rush gained from control leads to a need for more control, which provides a bigger rush — and the Deluded Lover is hooked into a destructive cycle.
3. Instead of learning to use drugs or alcohol, co-dependents learn to use people. But they suffer from the same uninformed denial that "trouble won't happen to me." (The rationale is that my behavior is eventually for everybody's good.)
4. When this new knowledge is integrated into the lifestyle, there is almost total and complete preoccupation. Everyone and everything is seen as possible to control.

5. Preoccupation with *self* is secret. ("If I do this in the exact right way, *self* will prosper and benefit.") Seeds of martyrdom and helplessness are secretly sown. When caught at the deception or confronted about their behavior, the controlling co-dependent is taken aback.

It's important here to emphasize that co-dependents' controlling and preoccupation with self is not a result of being "bad people." It is a result of their inability to feel, their attempts to meet genuine needs without knowing how to do so and their sincere denial.

**Denial**

Alcoholic denial is described by Robert Tarter, Ph.D., from Pittsburgh. One of the models of denial he describes is biopsychological. It fits co-dependents as well as chemical dependents.

The biopsychological approach considers denial a result of a physical and/or *chemical* defect that truly does not allow the individual to perceive or feel important signals from "their gut" or from the outside world. In order to support this theory, we must accept three hypotheses . . .

1. That alcoholics and dysfunctional family members are physiologically unstable in arousal regulation. There is no predictability or consistency in how they react to stress or stimulating experiences.
2. That alcoholics and other co-dependents cannot cognitively discriminate their "intereceptive" cues and physiological states. In other words, they *cannot* physically feel their feelings as completely as others.
3. That alcoholics and other co-dependents cognitively underestimate emotion-laden events in their lives and don't discuss those that they do notice.

In other words, they are unpredictable and unstable in terms of how much arousal or effect will come from an event that occurs around them and how much emotion will be attached to that event. They cannot in their minds' eye discriminate internal cues, such as changes in their pulse rate or respiration or heart rate, as signals that something is amiss. They are what many therapists call "numbed out."

They also underestimate and misinterpret events that are occurring around them. They underestimate the amount of emotion that is attached to their lives. They wonder, "What's the big deal?" And they don't discuss those events, but they do notice, "Geez, I feel badly about all this but I'm not going to let anybody know it!" Naturally, they and those around them have feelings of estrangement and detachment. There is a disconnected state separating and phasing them out as they deny their reality.

If we are in constant denial, we wear out our ability to think, to interpret, to feel and to put proper emphasis on emotional events that occur in our lives. Consequently, not having experienced these emotions to the degree that others have, we deny their significance or even their existence. Those around us who tend to believe us think they are crazy.

## Self-Deception

Self-deception has been the subject of scientific speculation for years. Freud explained it as one of our major defense mechanisms. He proposed that self-deception was repressing threatening information when it started to pass through the brain. Of course, he also thought that much of the information that was threatening to us evolved out of our own id or subconscious, and that it was the job of our conscience or superego to keep that information suppressed, to keep the lid on the boiling cauldron. Today many believe that boiling cauldron is not a burden, but rather is the emotions and feelings that originally needed recognition and expression rather than avoidance and suppression.

In recent years, we have been able to understand that people do deceive themselves and sidetrack the flow of information that may be going through their brain and reaching their consciousness. In certain situations this may even be helpful.

Certainly under pressure in a wartime experience, when one is caught in life-threatening situations, climbing mountains or crossing swollen rivers, a certain amount of denial is an aid to our performance as it allows our more primitive brains to take over and accomplish the task at hand.

There is one aspect of denial that is almost pre-denial in its form. In all of us there is a continuous assortment of huge amounts of information coming into the brain. Most of this cannot be used by the brain, and so only a small amount of what is reality actually gets up to the cortex and into consciousness. Our minds are constantly shutting out the sounds of refrigerators, cars going by, someone in the other room and so on. As the brain concentrates on a task or thought it loses the big picture of its surroundings and other events going on simultaneously.

When painful or anxiety-producing stimuli come in at a furious rate, as they do for someone living in an active alcoholic or drug-abusing home, the brain focuses elsewhere. Painful events and behavior are to be tuned out. When later asked to recall such things, we cannot because they were never allowed to come past our initial sensors. Such events never processed at the conscious, feeling or memory level of our brains (Disassociation).

Of course, most of denial comes from information that is misprocessed and misinterpreted. But if information never reaches the brain, it can receive no processing whatsoever.

What information do we have regarding denial, not only by an individual but by an entire family? They may go into an almost predictable and apparent conspiracy of denial. Therapists who treat families in which there is developmental disability, chemical dependency or other kinds of dysfunction, know well that some families obscure the problems that exist in a full cloud of denial. These families cling to their deceptions by many different methods, most of them similar to those of the individual. There is an implicit or explicit agreement that no one is to talk.

*Example.* One child might say to the other as they come home from school and prepare their own noon lunches, "Mommy must really be tired to be sleeping on the living room floor." And the answer comes back, "Yeah . . ."

Members of the same family will frequently have an agreement, most often an unspoken one, not to notice or to acknowledge certain events and certainly not to talk about problems going on in the family. Frequently a vague problem is sensed, but the fact that it might be a serious one, rooted in alcoholism or other chemical dependency, is left covered by the children. This is also true of the spouse.

### Group Think

Goldman mentions the concept of *group think* that exists in such families. Group Think is not actually premeditated, it just occurs. It can be better appreciated in the corporate family. If a Chief Executive Officer surrounds himself with many individuals who think as he does, then Group Think determines what is real and what is right. Repeated common conclusions can be bonding, but can also exclude reality. In their collective denial, chemically dependent and co-dependent families develop their own cohesiveness and impressions of uniqueness. This pervades generation to generation. They may feel quite distanced from each other and yet appear impenetrable to the outside world.

Goldman quotes psychologist Michael Callaway, who has found that the dangers of such kind of group thinking are greatest when there is a strong leader and a strong focus of attention by the group. This is very similar to the dynamics of the focus of attention on the alcoholic in the alcoholic family that is described by Stephanie Brown. Individuals in a group or a family feel that the group is not simply close-knit but very special. Frequently if the actively dependent family remains intact, they are also impenetrable.

No matter how mythical that closeness may actually be, individual members are quite unlikely to challenge the group's feelings of pride, closeness or interpretation of reality. Do not challenge this image.

Someone who can be a devil's advocate or arrange a formal intervention can break through this kind of denial that exists even when Group Think or Family Think is occurring. Usually the messenger is at risk of being shot, but if the message gets through, many get well together. If family members can risk confronting events, such as occurs in a formal intervention, they can break through individual and group denial. Then insight is gained, maybe temporarily, but recovery only needs a crack in the door to slip into a family. The results justify the risks.

## Repetitive Compulsive Behavior

When we recognize the recurring temporary benefits of repetitive compulsive behavior, co-dependency becomes a more understandable disease. Someone is trying to meet their needs and in doing so finds relief through medicating behaviors, medicating concepts and medicating substances. These all have brain effects. It's integrated deeply into the brain and remains there to be used over and over and over again, even inappropriately. The denial that's necessary to keep it there builds in its sophistication and its power. The entire process shapes our personality. The brain sends out "overload" messages as co-dependent thinking, denial and behavior expand.

What are some of the examples of co-dependent feelings that could be listed as symptoms and what are some examples of co-dependent behaviors that could be listed as signs? First of all, many of us who have co-dependency have decided long ago that there is *one and only*. That is *one and only ONE* right way of doing and being. We have in our mind that there is a way the world is to turn and what our role in the world is to be. There is nothing left to chance. Our problem is to figure out just exactly what the turning world should be doing and what our personal role is. We begin to experiment. We learn to test the water.

We are quickly caught up in a series of flirtations with different ways of behaving and thinking. Co-dependents test out the use of success and the use of power, the use of being cute, the use of being loud, the use of being quiet, the use of being in control (dependent) and the use of substances (addict). We learn the use of laudatory behaviors, such as excess work or caretaking behavior. We learn the use of procrastination, diversion and confusion (avoidant). We learn the use of crisis and drama and attention-getting behavior (histrionic).

We learn these things by trial and error, by simply deducing that they might work, based on our own past experiences or by what we have observed (Modeling). We use these experiences in exaggerated forms for easing our cravings for connectedness, for reality, for security.

As our disease progresses, we learn more and more means of reinforcement by initially experiencing relief or reward. We integrate these processes, not only in our brain, but into our lifestyle. So there are effects of our toxic behavior on our brains (signs and symptoms) and also there are now effects of our toxic behavior on our lives (complications).

Co-dependents can be so preoccupied with their own behavior, with their own thoughts, living in their own "headworld," that they meet the criteria of a Narcissistic Personality Disorder.

Co-dependents place high value on their own discoveries, and make sure they will be within an environment where their discoveries work best. Those of us who are co-dependent would not go to a confronting or totally healthy environment because most of our coping behaviors would not be allowed. We dissociate from those who are unlike us, and we continue our denial and delusion that what we have thus far accomplished is "The Way." Our delusion grows. Although there is a disassociation from the outside world into our own headworld, there is still enough awareness that behaviors which initially worked well may need changing. Even in a circle of fellow co-dependents, friends, associates and relatives, we might begin to stand out and appear abnormal if we insist on continuing certain behaviors.

Instead of stopping, we attempt to hide the behavior. We, like the alcoholic, begin our secret affair, our secret life, our secret obsessions and compulsions with behaviors that, we have become firmly convinced, provide the way.

## Rituals

Rituals are the primary tools of the co-dependent. Certain compulsive activities are perceived as normal. There is daily planning or fantasizing so that loss of control or the ability to exercise new control will happen appropriately. The control of others comes first. Co-dependents must remain deluded that they are not really losing control, that it is not happening to them. ("No one can criticize me for my intentions.")

## The Affair

By the time co-dependents are into their full-blown affair with their behavior and their co-dependency, they are changing their tactics and using their ingenuity so as not to be discovered.

We need alibis and lies to cover up our true agendas. We exaggerate. We are unable to discuss our failures and our anxieties or hide them from friends and family. We have problems needing to know just exactly when things will "turn our way again." We are always looking forward to a new energizing situation for which we may concoct or even exaggerate the problems to give us even more energy. Like addicts and alcoholics, we go through the loss of benefits that "it's no fun anymore," and we enter into the same similar repeat love/hate relationship with ourselves and what we are doing. It seems that our denial becomes greater when we are plummeting into deeper and deeper depths of difficulty with our relationships, our work and so forth. We continue to say to ourselves, "I can change without any help! . . . If I need to . . . I think . . ."

Lastly, a great driving force for a co-dependent to continue the same behavior over and over and over again, even in secret, is our intense fear of abandonment. If our private thoughts and private motivations behind our behavior are discovered, we will become less likeable, less lovable and, therefore, will be abandoned . . . left by ourselves.

**Co-dependency Symptoms And Signs**

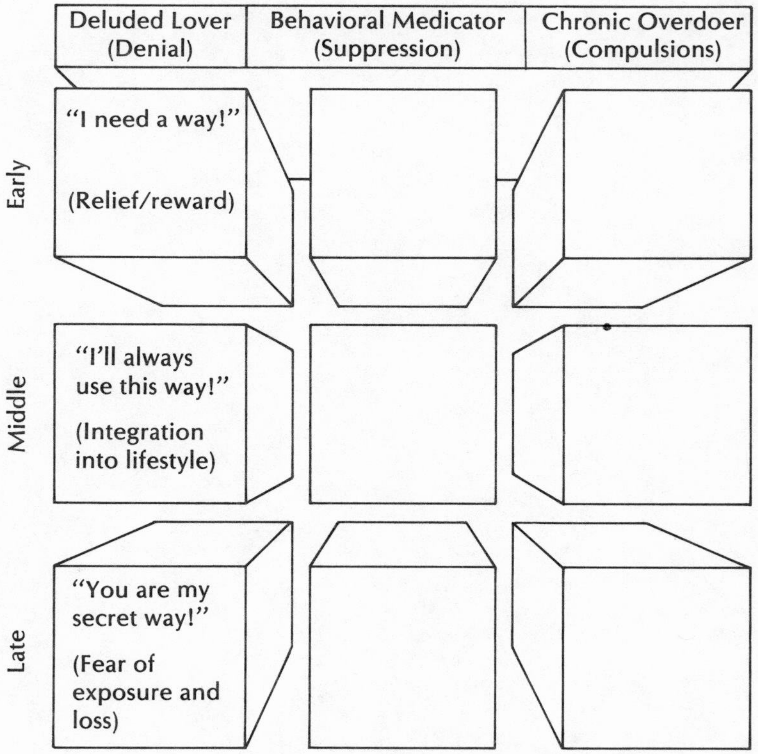


This is a description of the ***PRIMARY BRAIN*** disease of co-dependency, showing the major symptom groups of progressive delusion (denial), behavioral medicating and compulsive overdoing.

# 11

# Control By Suppression (Feelings)

## The Medicator

Feelings. How do feelings come about? Are they simply there to be controlled and suppressed and done away with if they are negative? Are they there to be exaggerated, stimulated and thoroughly enjoyed if they are positive? Is denial an actual loss of perception by an individual? Is someone who we say is *in denial* actually out of touch with reality? Can someone who is paying full attention to their emotions, sensations that are telling them what is genuine in the world, actually remain in denial? Or if someone is in denial, is it a requirement that they continuously suppress and ignore feelings and emotions to the extent that no actual picture of what's going on in their environment is available to them?

It takes constant effort and energy to suppress feelings and emotions if we are to maintain manufactured or outdated ideas and beliefs in our brain. Perhaps our outward belief has no use, but we have found it worked in the past and so, come hell or high water, we're going to hang on to it. Our behavior will reflect that idea or belief. The people around us begin to feel "crazy." We need a great deal of suppression of a lot of *other* signals coming in from our external and internal environment.

We are blessed with special senses that tell us what is going on in our general environment and immediately around us. They even give our brain and senses the capability of knowing what's going on around and outside our planet by using external data-gathering equipment, such as a radio, television or satellite. We are able to ascertain the weather, the political scene and other current happenings.

## The Five Senses

Our internal five senses give us a great deal of information regarding our external world. Those five senses are sight, sound, touch, taste and smell. All are used either individually or in concert with each other. We are almost always able to know whether or not our environment is friendly or hostile and whether we should *fight or flee or connect.*

Information from our skin, nose, tongue, ears and eyes is sent to separate centers in the brain, where it is processed and coordinated with information coming from within us. This information is then sent through the brain to higher centers into the neocortex, where old memories, old experiences, our belief systems, value system and our intelligence are allowed to act upon the information. It is modified by these centers as it reaches the more primitive midbrain where most chemicals for our emotions are stored. It then influences that midbrain to send certain combinations of chemicals and neurological signals throughout the body almost as a "shower" or a cascade of feelings. The result of all this information processing, which is almost instantaneous, is a feeling or emotion coupled with a thought. The sight of a long-term and dear friend, the smell of a rose, the touch of a loved one, the taste of a gentle spice or the sound of music can stimulate a pleasant, sad or nostalgic shower of natural body chemicals.

Sometimes our feelings seem to have no basis. We may have anxiety with no obvious cause present or fears in surroundings that to all intents and purposes are totally benign and passive. Sometimes these are old suppressed or otherwise unanswered feelings. They result in free-floating anxiety of our gut feelings.

## The Sixth Sense

We locate many of our feelings in the area of the trunk of the body, especially the epigastrium or the stomach area. Chemicals that influence feelings can also influence heart rate, respiration rate, muscle tension or tone, plus the sensitivity and perceptiveness of our five basic senses. It is possible that when we say "I have a gut feeling about something," we are actually using a *sixth sense.*

We never have accurately identified or defined what is meant by our sixth sense. We often place great importance on it, however. It may provide our only basis for making decisions without solid data or evidence. Our emotions and feelings may serve as the basis for our greatest risk-taking. Perhaps the value of our feelings is to signal us in situations where our other five senses do not provide quite enough data for us to use.

As we grow, we are instructed to set aside or control our emotions.

"Don't cry like a baby." "Big boys don't cry." "It's not nice to be angry." "Don't show anger. You may embarrass or frighten people." Statements that we have grown up with lead us to the belief that emotions are a burden for us to bear and have little practical use except for the superficial emotions of joy and laughter, etc.

"Always have your cute smile ready," is a mixed message that we have a nice smile, but our feelings come secondary to our mission: appear pleasant to favorably impress others.

"People don't like grouches" is another message that tells us we must maintain at least an outward demeanor of happiness, joy and having it all together. Being scolded for natural emotional reactions is quite commonplace in dysfunctional or alcoholic families. Feelings are discouraged, and a family member is a problem if they are unable to control their feelings.

When a person growing up in such a family finds a suppressive or divertive alternative to their negative feelings or finds a way of otherwise temporarily denying those negative feelings and therefore finding relief, they say to their brain, "Brain, I have found it, this is the answer, don't forget it! Remember, when something like this happens again, react in the same manner. Reward and relief will come again and again!"

And so when painful feelings keep bubbling to the surface, they require suppression. We find some sort of compulsive and frenetic activity, work or busyness and accomplishment that pushes those emotions down to where they no longer hurt or hurt as much.

When we face an emotional task associated with negative emotions, such as letting someone know that we consider ourselves injured and are angry about it, we use avoidant measures to skirt around the problem. Total acceptance of another's behavior that is affecting us or our loved ones is a form of avoiding unpleasant feelings. In situations where showing our emotions is justified, we tend to accept a neutralist reaction to the situation. Our stance is punctuated with two words, "Oh well . . ."

In addition to suppressing or denying feelings, some of us learn to medicate by the use of mind- and mood-altering drugs. Alcohol and nicotine temporarily avoid and "anesthetize" our feeling self first, our psychological self second and our physical self third. Eating, gambling and sexual acting-out can maintain a diversion from the existence of painful feelings. Many reinforcing, rewarding and relieving behaviors result in an actual imprint in the brain that says, "This is the way. There is no other way. You've got to totally and completely keep yourself under control and *at ready,* like a soldier, to face any situation which may come up. You must be vigilant at all times!"

**Brain Reactions**

Even after totally painful messages are received, the brain will continue to react in its original imprinted way. The brain can be told that everything is all right and even though it won't respond with chemicals of joy, it will not respond with chemicals of despair and pain. It will also stop receiving certain impulses so that it can maintain itself in a state of denial. It must create and concoct stories to explain the environment, regardless of the data that is coming into it from the other five senses and from the sixth sense, our feelings and emotions. The brain apparently is able to do this well if we use it in this manner.

Feelings are a sixth sense. Denial suppresses and represses these feelings, one of our major senses.

We have a physical life that is sometimes pleasant, sometimes painful and sometimes both at once. Our acceptance that our feelings are for our benefit, rather than something to be controlled or suppressed, helps to arm us for episodes of emotional pain or pleasure. Our emotions are not always the result of what happens to us, but they may be reality signaling and guiding us. Our subsequent behavior predicts where our feelings will be. When changed for our benefit in a positive manner, it will result in positive feelings.

We learn to believe in the importance of physical pain when we use it to signal proper behavior, such as taking an aspirin, resting the painful part or seeking medical help. The goal of this behavior is usually relief and prevention of further difficulty or disease. We also learn through painful feelings. We learn to rest or seek professional help. So both emotional and physical feelings, when heeded, result in appropriate behavior which in turn results in positive emotional and physical feelings.

Freedom lies in understanding our feelings and being able to act on that understanding. Assertive behavior, such as specifically directed anger, prevents aggressive behavior which may be randomly directed.

***Assertive behavior protects one's rights and feelings and develops a sense of self-worth. Aggressive behavior attacks someone else and attacks their worth, their rights and their feelings.***

For those diseases which are emotionally based, psychiatrically based, cognitively based, developmentally based or metabolically based, our feelings are the tools. Our feelings are our cues to the disorders that may exist within us and are our access to the recovery we can expect.

As co-dependents we must learn not only to suppress feelings, but to become expert at it. We have assumed numerous survival roles to cover up feelings, are driven by a fear of abandonment and have embraced a manner of believing and behaving because of our problems with identity. Just as the addict uses drugs to medicate feelings, we achieve a similar result by suppressing feelings.

## Medicating Behaviors

A behavior that serves to reinforce us with relief or reward can be considered a "Medicating Behavior." Medicating behaviors can be so all-consuming that they actually have many of the characteristics of an addiction, which usually requires ever-increasing amounts and frequency of use.

Pathological and dependent relationships require increasing intensity, usually in the form of crisis. They require increasing frequency, usually in the form of dependency. They require increasing variety, usually in the form of impulsiveness and quick changes. Without these increases, benefits are lost. Sound like an alcoholic?

Negative reinforcement, which is in essence relief that is obtained from the use of alcohol and drugs, can also be obtained in other ways. There are behaviors which give both positive and negative enforcement.

## Negative Reinforcement

First, we'll look at those which give negative reinforcement, in other words *relief* from emotional pain. We have spoken about drugs, alcohol, nicotine and sugar as chemical medicators we use to suppress or otherwise change chronic emotional pain. These behaviors which medicate emotional pain and are most commonly used by co-dependents are frequently ones that result in serious abuse of some of our natural instincts and drives. One of these is Sexuality Abuse, not sexual abuse, but *sexuality* abuse.

### *Sexuality Abuse*

We have our own God-given powers for sensuousness and sexual feelings and sexual behavior. When this is used to excess and for the purpose of suppressing anxiety, depression and other painful emotions, we are then abusing a natural characteristic about ourselves. Sexuality abuse is also frequently used as a temporary "upper" in terms of having affairs.

The "high" from sexuality abuse can come from the excitement of a new relationship. It's the chase! And the chase is on! The conquest has begun! Attack! Thrust! Parry! Chide! Coddle! Share! Plead! Use techniques that are hopefully new. Win the day! And the penis and the vagina become an anticlimactic momentary surge of sensations. Then . . . the rush is over and the orgasm quickly flattens, bringing us down to the next stage, emotional negativity.

Sensuality, sexuality and sexual acting out are not used as the intended extension and catalyst of an established mature love of two human beings for one another. Rather, post-orgasmic and post-conquest disregard and disdain for the partner may exist. The partner turns out to be quite a different person. Body attributes, charm, likableness, admiration and openness are not as attractive as they seemed to be before the conquest. Frequently any pre-orgasmic thoughts of commitment and long-range planning lose their sheen, but the intensity of the moment begets another.

To guarantee the next event, extra patience, extra effort, extra concoctions and expressions of care and concern are used where needed. Even after the initial "glow" has worn off, such arrangements are often put "on hold" rather than cancelled. It's almost like being prepared for an "emergency erection" or a sudden attack of "pure skin hunger." "Never be without a supply" is the motto of the alcoholic and drug addict also.

### *Eating Abuse*

Another abuse of our normal bodily functions is eating. So much emotion is innately connected with our skin and our mouth, so much positive reinforcement occurred for us as infants that it is difficult not to use that established "feel good" circuit of placing something to eat in our mouth for immediate, even though temporary surcease from emotional pain. Eating . . . and eating . . . and eating. And for some, sugar gives an extra surge for a moment but it, too, takes its toll.

### *Exercise Excess*

A third example of excessive use or abuse of one of our body's abilities is that of jogging or exercising or body-building. Exercise is often carried to a degree of intensity that results in a chemical rush. The rush comes from reaching a certain oxidative state of exercise and this can be combined with the rush of pride from viewing one's own body becoming more attractive to society or the opposite sex.

### *Workaholism*

Other means of medicating our negative emotions are those of becoming superheroes at accomplishing. We can medicate our negative emotions by excessive busyness to the point of workaholism, to the point of ignoring our world around us, including the valuable people in it. Gambling is a means of "rushing" our body so that it eventually becomes more gratifying to place the bet than to make any kind of a win with it, unless it's an excessively big win.

Natural function medicators such as sexuality and food abuse, and additional medicators of work, gambling, accomplishing, avoiding, controlling and accumulating are all accompanied by significant amounts of tolerance.

Just as with other types of repetitive behavior, our physical body, especially our brain, becomes imprinted with the behavior, ceasing to give us any kind of emotional response. To go for the emotional response, we must, therefore, either go for the "rush" or the "steady state" which now requires increasing frequency, increasing intensity, increasing duration and increasing variety to obtain and maintain our sense of well-being or super-being.

## Brain Shutdown

At this point, the brain becomes somewhat overwhelmed (or perhaps the word should be underwhelmed) and begins to shut down. Feelings disappear. Reality, as expressed by feelings, begins to abate and a false reality or a separation from feelings, as described earlier, begins to occur. And just as the alcoholic or addict is required to go "underground" to maintain their practices and avoid discovery, so must the co-dependent to maintain their increasingly unacceptable behavior. They also need to go underground and hope not to be found out. The behaviors continue to increase in intensity, frequency and variety.

If this behavior is suddenly stopped, it is not unlike the sudden stopping of drugs. Anxiety, fear, sense of loss and a lowering of self-worth begin to happen. The person immediately restarts the behavior to avoid these painful feelings. There is almost a constant need for the behavior on a regular and steady basis to avoid these sensations or feelings of withdrawal, of doing nothing, of being nothing.

## Tolerance Build Up

A workaholic who finally gets promoted needs a bigger promotion. A sexuality abuser after a conquest needs two more conquests. An eating abuser needs to double the amounts or kinds and episodes of eating for the same effect. For some reason, we develop tolerance to both chemicals *and* behaviors. We gain fewer benefits with each use or occurrence. This can result in anxiety or depression. We need to continually increase the *intensity* of an activity, such as an affair, or increase the frequency and the *duration* of an activity, such as eating. Then we need to increase the combinations of activities, such as work and accumulation, and later, work and accumulation plus status.

As a person begins to learn behaviors, thoughts and ideas to control their emotions and feelings, certain other events take place that are quite well known to those with chemical addictions. It is the problem of tolerance.

Tolerance arises even to behaviors, ideas and concepts. For instance, a person who is a workaholic may be working overtime and getting rewarded both monetarily and by praise in the office. After a time the praise wears thin and begins to sound hollow, and the extra income isn't doing all those things that it originally appeared to do. The person must increase either the frequency of the behavior they're performing or add additional behaviors to it to get the original sensation of reward or relief that they sought in the first place.

Most of the time we see people simply increasing frequency, duration and intensity. It's the same whether it is sexual affairs, whether it is gambling, whether it is work, whether it is accomplishing goals or obtaining material things. Co-dependents are driven to greater and greater duration, frequency and intensity.

In addition, they are chronically and constantly searching for variety as a means of coping. The alternatives, they find, can be equally disturbing and destructive.

An example of this addictive behavior might be that of the person who is constantly and chronically abusing his sexuality to find that the rush is less and the let-down is greater than when he first began that behavior. Therefore, he has to add drugs or alcohol to enhance the rush, either the orgasmic rush or the rush that comes with the chase and the conquest.

Many of the characteristics of the co-dependent person or the child from an alcoholic or otherwise dysfunctional family evolve from the continuous need to increase duration or frequency and intensity and varieties of behavior. Characteristics that may result are ongoing chronic patterns of intense, but unstable, relationships. On occasion, there is hero worship and hero envy plus pedestal-placing. This is followed by criticism, devaluation and disdainful attitudes. Frequently there are more and more shifts in mood from depression to excitement, from irritability to joy, from anxiety to apathy. Large swings in mood accompany periods of let down when an individual realizes that relief or the reward was only temporary. There are chronic feelings of emptiness or boredom as one becomes used to and resistant or tolerant to their own behavior. Frantic efforts to attempt to increase the previously received rewards and relief fall short and shorter and shorter.

## Self-Damaging Behaviors

Impulsiveness can be extremely self-damaging if an individual attempts to add additional behaviors to the already intense and frequent behaviors they have been using for their rushes. Spending, reckless driving, eating, smoking, thrill-seeking and crisis creation are all means of avoiding emotional reality. Suppressing and diverting oneself from true emotional reality becomes an art, not unlike the art of juggling. Sadly there is little rest and respite if all the balls must be kept flying and if self-worth and fear of discovery depend on not dropping a single ball.

Even when people start to sense that they are involved in many nonproductive and actually damaging behaviors, they cannot seem to stop. When they find they're no longer receiving even short-lived benefits that were welcomed in the past, when they find that they have become a slave to their own compulsive behaviors, they naturally want to change or temper those behaviors. But the emotional pain of withdrawing from those behaviors seems to be even greater than continuing them.

Therefore, the co-dependents continue in an impulsive and compulsive fashion with the behaviors that are now designed to simply stabilize or prevent further discomfort for them. They continue the same behavior just in order to feel "normal." This is not unlike alcoholics whose tolerance has driven them beyond stronger and more frequent and more bizarre combinations. It is not unlike the alcoholic who is just doing miserable maintenance drinking to stay ahead of withdrawal. Just drinking. This is not realistic either in its design to neutralize or prevent negative emotions, and it becomes clearly excessive in its nature, consuming a significant portion of the person's waking hours.

By this time, the co-dependent jugglers are becoming exhausted from the effort of keeping all those balls in the air. It isn't fun anymore. They wake up in the mornings with no energy for the day. They feel fatigued and unmotivated. There may be significant loss of appetite, perhaps loss of sleep or a need for excessive sleep. The person may feel sad and slow to laugh and have difficulty in concentrating. They begin to wonder if they can actually survive much longer. At one moment there may be a feeling of close attachment, complete trust and love toward someone. Later, maybe devaluing them, becoming critical and judgmental. As tolerance increases and withdrawal depression becomes more intense, there can be marked instability in moods.

### Behavior Addiction

Now irritability, anxiety and increased motor activity almost seem to be necessary. The person's preoccupation with a way of behaving becomes more intense. The preoccupation with self and with, "How is it going to be today for me?" begins to build, along with the intensity, duration, frequency and varieties of coping behavior. There comes a point when the person is totally and completely embroiled in and addicted to certain sets of behaviors. These initially provided some sort of reinforcement in the form of relief or reward, but now they are so imprinted that to cease them is unthinkable and will only result in withdrawal depression. Even if the person is given a bit of insight and a lot of knowledge, they cannot stop their behavior, as much as they would like to.

An example might be a workaholic who for years has worked Saturdays and Sunday mornings, claiming that Sunday afternoon was his time off. Sunday afternoon, however, he would come home and continue phoning and putting "deals" together. The kids and the wife would sit by. Suppose this workaholic realizes and decides he no longer wishes to do that. He may find that although this level of behavior is no longer giving him benefit, he has developed tolerance to it.

The rewards and suppression of feelings that used to go with it are no more. Feelings are beginning to escape when he tries to stop his compulsive behavior. Extreme anxiety, tension and actual physical changes may occur as he enters workaholism withdrawal of such severity that only professional help can provide safe and complete detoxing. Recovery can then begin. It's not unlike detoxing a patient who is physically dependent on alcohol or another drug, who needs to endure the withdrawal syndrome before the other aspects of the disease of chemical dependency can be treated and a full recovery can begin.

**Withdrawal**

We've all experienced the letdown or the "withdrawal" that occurs after a great victory, promotion, birthday celebration, buying a new car, etc. This is normal and natural, and usually we handle it well. Co-dependents believe in, and even expect, momentary rewards. They trust the meager "here and now" over the grand "perhaps one day." They learned this long ago. When ever-multiple meager rewards are removed, they suffer a psychological withdrawal. It causes a frenetic searching for a solution or a substitute, similar to the drug- or alcohol-seeking behavior seen in a chemically dependent person.

Research in the chemistry of the brain and studies of the learning process have begun to demonstrate how all this works in our brains. There is an actual chemical mechanism called reinforcement, based on a substance called dopamine from the base of our midbrain, which results in the flooding of our bodies with certain chemicals that make us feel positive, either relieved or rewarded. In addition we're learning more and more about the concept of denial and how positive reinforcement (reward) or negative reinforcement (relief) can be maintained in the brain by denial against all obvious evidence. No matter what the environment might be telling the brain through its intellect, feelings and five senses, the brain is able to ignore and suppress that data.

The signals of reality from our gut and our outside world go to our conscious brain and we sanely and rationally react with our imprinted behaviors. If our intellect and our rational logic mind is not fed conflicting information, it will remain out of conflict. Many children from alcoholic and other dysfunctional families acquire a great talent for denying.

Intereceptive (inner) signals from our body are usually accurate pieces of information regarding our current condition. They register as feelings. We learn to suppress these pieces of reality by ceasing to respond to our feelings. We then lack intuition. Exteroceptive (outer) signals from our environment are usually accurate pieces of information also. They register through our five senses of taste, touch, smell, seeing and hearing.

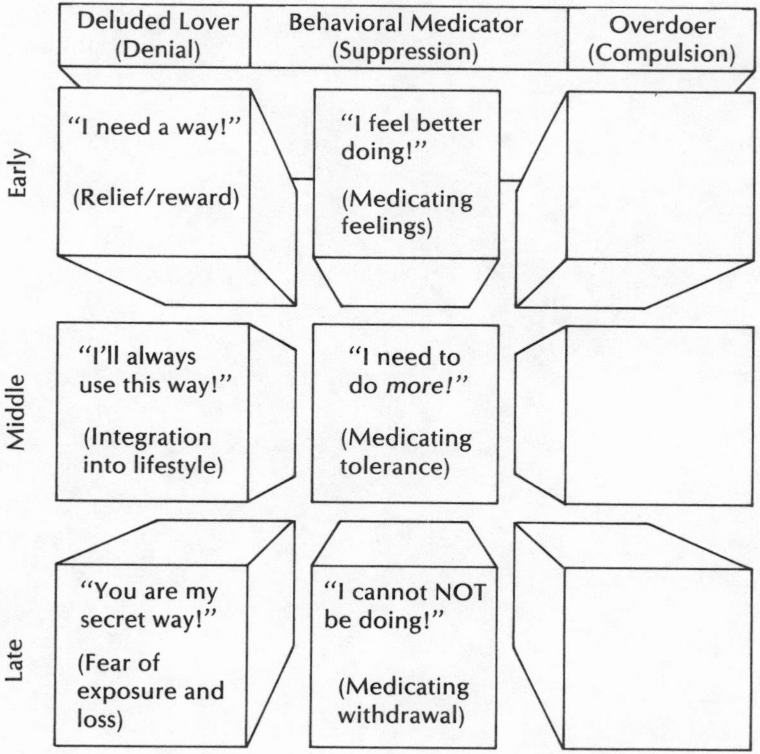


This is a description of the ***PRIMARY BRAIN*** disease of co-dependency, showing the major symptom groups of progressive delusion (denial), behavioral medicating and compulsive overdoing.

12

# Control By Compulsions (Behaviors)

## The Overdoer

The signs and symptoms and especially the complications that occur in co-dependency are shockingly similar to the signs and symptoms of chemical dependency. The major differences are the excessive use and the serious effects of alcohol and other drugs in chemical dependency. The major similarities between the diseases are the yearning and striving for relief, reward, recognition, connection, spirituality, intimacy, emotional peace, personal freedom, personal rights and personal choices.

We all have needs, fears, urgings and cravings. When we learn to satisfy them, even briefly, temporarily or dysfunctionally, the brain is *reinforced* through *relief* or *reward.*

***Reinforcement is a process whereby the brain believes that the event which led up to the relief or the reward will always lead up to a reward or relief.***

When a susbstance or a behavior is said to be "highly reinforcing," it refers to the high probability that such a substance or behavior will be repeated again and again . . . even well beyond the time that the original benefits cease. Reinforcing events can be in the form of an idea, recognition of an accomplishment, winning a contest, imbibing alcohol or using mind-altering drugs, falling in love and many others.

**Personality Reinforcement**

Events that reinforce one person do not necessarily reinforce another. Alcohol is much, much more reinforcing to an alcoholic than it is to a non-alcoholic. Apparently our age, our genes, our prior history, our beliefs and our environment have a great influence in determining how much reinforcement we get from the various events that occur in our lives. These reinforcements become a part of our *personhood* as they are integrated into our brain centers and our belief, memory and value systems. Accuracy isn't necessarily a requirement for the brain to accept the information.

Once this information is integrated into our brain, it becomes a routine manner of behaving. Now it is a part of our lifestyle and our thinking. It becomes a part of our *personality.* This personality begins to have difficulty with the other personalities it loves and wants to love. Because of our great fear of abandonment and of being discovered in what might be considered marginal or abnormal behavior or thinking, it becomes necessary to cover up and not risk discovery. "I can't let you know the real me . . . you won't like me . . ."

When a dysfunctional lifestyle goes on long enough, it becomes entrenched or imprinted within the individual. Repeated ongoing dysfunctional reinforcing results in a loss of reality, especially as feelings are suppressed and avoided more and more. We begin to doubt our own identity — we as an individual are not fully developed. We are still a child in some dimensions of our personality (Brown, Subby). Another dynamic in the evolving disease of co-dependency is in place.

Because of genetics, excessive or repetitive behavior or chronic stress (which many co-dependents actually confuse with excitement), co-dependent behavior stimulates the brain to provide certain chemicals for energy, for a "hyper" feeling, for a euphoric feeling. Co-dependent behaviors result in the look-alike feelings of joy and happiness that are only temporary.

The stress signal goes out to and from the brain again that all is not well. The irresistible cravings, fears and urgings send a signal to the co-dependent brain to again begin the chaos, the stress, the look-alike excitement. The brain becomes overloaded — efficient functioning diminishes. Another temporary stopgap.

Have we learned enough about the chemistry of the brain to say that compulsive behavioral disease and perhaps other mental diseases such as bipolar depression and schizophrenia are chemically based in the brain? More and more evidence for this is being uncovered daily.

## Repression And Denial

There is also evidence that the brain actually uses a process of repressing information, sometimes for the benefit and sometimes to the detriment of the individual. This repression appears on the surface to others as denial. Learned repression is used when nothing can be done to change a perceived threat, when one is powerless. Then panic can be avoided for the moment by denying or blocking out the perception of powerlessness. In some cases denial becomes an effective means to stay relatively calm and therefore better able to save ourselves.

Denial can entail physical risks, such as tuning out danger signals from chest or abdominal pains. Addiction or alcoholism have their own forms of denial in tuning out severity or consequences. Co-dependency denial tunes out situations and reality. Some people are described as "repressors" (Goldman). Repressors seem to have either been born with the ability or acquired the technique of avoiding upsetting information. This can be a survival tool for a child avoiding unbearable emotional pain.

Denial certainly is present in an alcoholic family, where severe problems are totally ignored. Individuals in such a family begin to block their own senses. They can, in fact, cancel out specific and realistic information coming from their senses, including their feelings. There is a state of complete chaos as far as the person's thinking and hearing are concerned. The self-protection of medicating or suppressing negative emotions becomes ingrained into the individual's brain. In essence, the brain is told, "Don't forget it!" The brain is told, "It worked this time and it will probably always work."

## Delusions

The world is not making sense, but the deluded brain can with its own pseudo-logic. People's delusions require constant "talking" to themselves, convincing themselves and discounting the outside world and the information it is sending.

This person certainly becomes somewhat tenuous in their own self-confidence and ability to make decisions. As problems become more complex and the continuing denial requires more complex solutions, the person begins to doubt their own intuition, their own feelings, their own ability to think, their own intelligence and especially their own memory.

Cermak and Brown identified the mistrust of one's own perceptions and the mistrust of others as one of the key issues they noticed in the earlier phases of their group therapy treatment for alcoholics. Since there is denial of factual data coming through our five senses, there is also denial of the emotions that are coming through from both external and internal stimuli. Denying one's feelings is probably denying reality.

Maintaining an erroneous belief system at all costs requires increasing efforts. By now the co-dependent person is overdosing with toxic behaviors, such as creative lying and/or toxic *levels* of behaviors which in themselves are not necessarily harmful. When the behaviors are increased in frequency, intensity and duration, they do become toxic. As they strive to maintain medicating levels of behavior, co-dependents become increasingly rigid and controlling. In truth, they become less than desirable personality types in our society. As their reality becomes more and more distorted and their behavior to maintain that reality more and more exaggerated, certain sets of symptoms begin to appear. These can be identified as co-dependency symptoms or, in the more extreme and bizarre forms, specific psychiatric disorders.

## Passive-Aggressive Behavior

Passive-aggressive behavior becomes an efficient means of controlling existing perceptions and beliefs. It also helps not to have to give credence to anyone else's opinions or even give them an opportunity to express their opinions. "A good offense is a good defense." People begin to show resistance to demands made on them by the real world — socially, occupationally and in their interpersonal relationships. This resistance may take the form of procrastination, not meeting deadlines and being constantly late, controlling by maintaining irritation and chaos secondary to this.

Other passive-aggressive behaviors include our being constantly irritable, argumentative and angry, or assuming or attempting to complete a job, but doing it extremely slowly or badly so that it must be repeated. The passive-aggressive person is a chronic "whiner" who protests without justification, except to themselves, that others are making unreasonable demands on them. There is beginning difficulty with memory. Then there are the fictitious memory lapses that in truth are simply means of controlling when no loss of memory actually occurred.

Most of the time these people feel they are justified. They believe they are successful in their relationships and their work, but the world just does not understand them or is not able to see how well they are really doing. Therefore, they resent any attempt to help, quick to turn it aside and obstruct the efforts of others, even when it does not involve them directly. There is usually a sense of scorn and anger toward authority figures. The anger is highly controlled, however, because of the fear of showing one's "true colors" as aggressive and angry.

By being able to control their perception of reality and the amount of data coming in that might cause them to have to change their perception of reality, these people maintain a steady, if somewhat, painful state. Feelings of anger frequently are simply manifestations and means of control. Anger is threatening, and individuals and society worry that anger may lead to destruction and rage. However, on occasion, anger is the only emotion that someone is able to show, and with it they can control and dominate others. Anger is a bona fide emotion and one that needs expression in a form of assertiveness to actually avoid aggression.

**Distorted Control**

As the distorted reality increases, the person becomes more and more controlling and can avoid reality by histrionic or excessive emotionality and attention-seeking. Those who are doing this maintain an avoidance and cause those around them to "shape up," pay attention and provide constant approval and reassurance and praise. Histrionic individuals particularly use their sexuality to maintain their sense of self-worth and importance and to avoid looking at any central issues that might be emotionally painful. They prefer to associate with individuals who are overly concerned with physical attractiveness and who exaggerate their expression of caring and greeting. They may show excessive ardor toward casual acquaintances.

Those who are becoming more and more out of touch with reality, centering on self, living entirely in their own headworld, are also self-centered and demanding of immediate satisfaction. They have no tolerance for delayed gratification. They are uncomfortable in situations in which they are not the center of attention and are impressionistic and overly dramatic.

Individuals who become so ingrained in their own headworld that they no longer consider the possibility the real world is different from what they perceive, get further and further into brain toxicity to the point that they react to any kind of confrontation or criticism with rage or by shaming or humiliation. They are grandiose in their behaviors and want to be noticed as special. They really, truly feel underneath that their problems are unique, that they have the right answer, that they are special in God's eyes, that they are here for a special purpose.

These persons begin to fantasize about unlimited control and unlimited success and brilliance and accomplishment with no basis. Because they are unable to perceive their own reality, nothing is impossible. They have a sense of entitlement, an unreasonable expectation of deserving especially favorable treatment. They assume they do not have to wait in line, for instance, when others do, or if they do have to wait, it's an imposition on them. These people become so preoccupied that they are hypervigilant, always watching, always on guard. They are on guard for any kind of transgression, but they are also on guard for any kind of applause, caring, nurturing or loving. They are very careful and very selective in any one who is allowed to get close to them. Most of the time they involve themselves in rapidly shifting up-and-down type relationships. Reality is kept in check so well that the person actually loses any empathy for those around them. They are unable to recognize how others feel, are frequently thought of as inconsiderate, and yet it's not their fault. They do not understand the effect or the impact of their impositions on others.

As all this progresses, it's easy to see how their "unreal self" becomes their "real self." Their unreal self is unable to get the basic needs for intimate attachment and comfort and self-worth met. They frequently begin to show chronic extended periods of depression, alternating with anxiety and hyper-manic behavior. As their fantasies and self-constructed headworld progress, they sometimes can leave reality totally and end up in mental institutions with one of the major psychoses. And it all started with the brain being told that "what works, works." And "what isn't, isn't" and "always listen to me."

Early on this is a matter of the brain losing some of its most valuable capabilities: Vigilance, perspective, memory, imagination, reality-based logic, insight and steady concentration. All of this is replaced with rigidity and dichotomous thinking that everything has to be black and white. "Everything has to be my way." "I have this figured out, I know what is real, you don't." Denial is telling one's brain, "This can't happen, this is not happening and, therefore, does not exist." Black-and-white thinking is "if something isn't bad, then it's good," or "if something isn't good, it's bad." There are no grays.

**Loss of Choice**

As the deluded and toxic brain continues on its course of denial and rigid logic to explain the reason for the world, it progresses to the point where there is a loss of reality and a loss of choice. Even when an individual is offered a choice of how they will think or behave, they no longer can choose. Once they ingrain a certain thinking pattern, they can no longer stop. Once they begin a certain behavior pattern, they can no longer stop.

Even though they may go to treatment centers or a therapist and "act as if," often they can only abstain from that kind of thinking and behavior for short periods of time. Recovery can only take place with some internal, affective and spiritual access and conversion. That access into the deepest parts of the person is necessary so that changes will be integrated, accepted and afterward used on a permanent basis. Otherwise the disease progresses further, with additional new traumas which need suppressing.

Our traumas from painful relationships, abuse, catastrophes or simply from a general lifestyle of chaos, start causing continual stress that is exemplified by the post-traumatic stress syndrome. Where there is now recurrent, continuing and intrusive distress, recollection of events that need suppression begins. This recollection often occurs in flashbacks, triggered by events in the present that are reminders of past pain. These can cause intense distress. The person feels and acts as if the previous traumatic event were happening again, experiencing all the attendant anxiety, fear of abandonment and fear of destruction. The person's entire day can be taken up with thoughts of how to avoid feelings or memories of such trauma.

## Anxiety And Paranoia

Caught up in the pain, someone feels a difference or estrangement from others. They have a restricted range of feelings, beginning to realize they can't feel love or be loved. There is a sense of foreboding and of impending doom — perhaps a career, marriage or children or a long life are not going to be granted to them. With this kind of ongoing tension and stress, there is irritability and difficulty concentrating, hyper-vigilance and an exaggerated startle response.

As they get further away from reality without actually becoming psychotic, these persons may share symptoms of expecting to be exposed to harm by others, becoming paranoid, reading hidden messages and meanings into newspaper articles or comments by others, continuing to carry grudges and resentments, being unforgiving, failing to confide in others and feeling easily slighted without any basis.

Individuals may reach the point where they desire no close relationships, that it is too much of a struggle for them. They would rather choose solitary activities and do not share any strong emotions one way or another. Their affect begins to diminish both from the negative and the positive standpoint, showing no joy or anger. They indicate little desire or interest in sexual experiences and they isolate socially and at work. They appear to others as aloof and cold with a sharp facial expression. As the disease progresses even further, excessive social anxiety and odd beliefs and thinking occur. Behavior that is inconsistent with the cultural norms — suspicions, odd behavior and odd appearance and dress, no close friends or confidants, and inappropriate or constricted affect may be present.

By this time the co-dependent person is striving mightily to hold it all together. The effort necessary to medicate and continually deny painful feelings, and to try to keep the environment totally under control, becomes almost too much. The complications of the disease are becoming an increasing factor in their life.

## Co-Dependency Symptoms And Signs

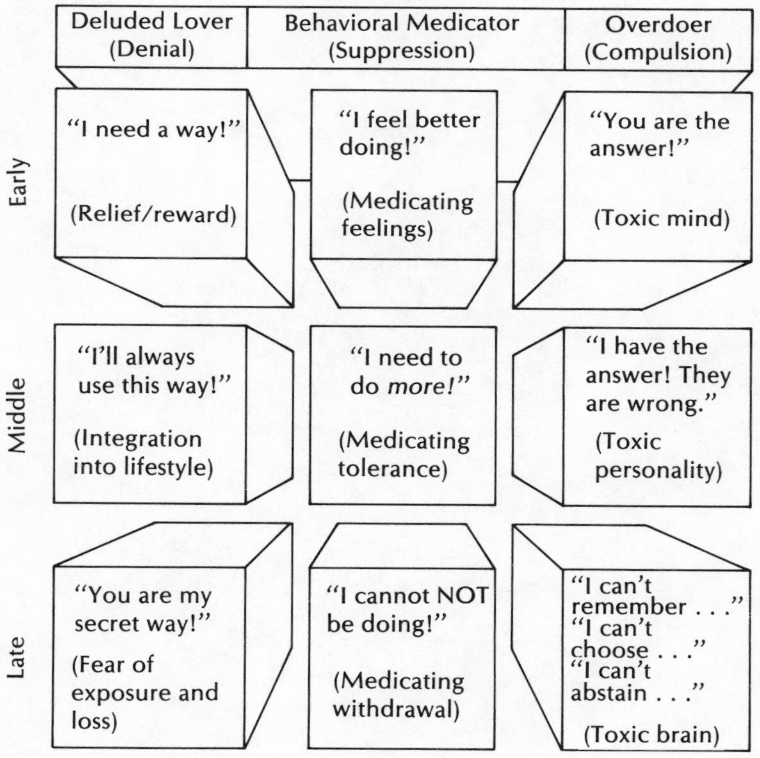


This is a summary of the ***PRIMARY BRAIN*** disease of co-dependency, showing the major symptom groups that result from the disease affecting the person's ***BRAIN.***

## 13

# Complications Of Co-dependency

In describing the diseases of both chemical dependency and co-dependency, we have grouped the descriptive symptoms and signs into those of a deluded and obsessive Lover, a suppressing self-medicator and a compulsive and imprisoned Overdoser. These three categories describe the effects of the disease on the individual's brain.

The complications described for the chemically dependent person, which are those events occurring in the life of a person with untreated chemical dependency, also hold true as descriptive groupings for co-dependency.

The first group consists of low self-worth, spiritually discontented *Loners.* The second group is the battling and conflicted *Warriors.* The third grouping for description is the early-aging, poor-functioning, organ-damaged *Relics.*

A review of the complications of chemical dependency reveals that almost all of the listed complications are generic in nature. Any disease allowed to go untreated and to progress even to death will have the same grouping of complications associated with it. Any disease in its advanced stages can be described as a bio-psycho-social-spiritual disease, and indeed both chemical dependency and co-dependency are such diseases.

## Loner

Co-dependents in recovery, as often as addicts and alcoholics in recovery, describe the severe state of loneliness and uniqueness that they feel. They have the same vague spiritual desires, low self-worth and questions of the value of life. Their brain becomes turned in rather than turned out to the world about them, and they become grandiose and self-absorbed. Suicide, remorse, helplessness and shame all play a great part. As a matter of fact, shame probably is the actual catalyst for the disease of co-dependency to continue.

Shame has been described by John Bradshaw as the basis of co-dependency. As a reactive and learned behavior, it is probably more a result of untreated co-dependency. In either case, it is absolutely important because of its ability to provide energy and drive to increasing and continuing co-dependent behavior. Shame is probably the link in the unending chain that forms a vicious circle. And just as it does in the isolated, humorless and helpless chemically dependent person in the later stages of their disease, suicide can become the final means of control and ultimate way out.

## Warrior

The perception that there is only one way of behaving and accomplishing and being causes distress, not only in the family, but in the workplace and society. Controlling behavior is most evident and best kept under wraps in the family setting. But controlling behavior can actually be taken advantage of in the workplace by employers who need strong managers and supervisors whose entire self-worth is wrapped up in how well they can control. Social conflicts with friends and neighbors, financial and even legal conflicts are common for the person with advanced co-dependency, as they are for the person with advanced chemical dependency.

**Relic**

Through learning about brain chemistry and understanding the effects of stress, anxiety and other external pressures on the body's normal homeostasis, it is no surprise that co-dependency can result in as many and varied physical effects as the actual intake of foreign chemicals and substances as seen in chemical dependency. The ability of our emotions, especially if suppressed, to influence our blood pressure, our heart, our immune system, our bones and joints, and our muscular system, is truly amazing. Our bodies have built such sophisticated sensory systems that we can indeed suffer from advanced and severe life-threatening physical illnesses because of our emotional state. The co-dependent, in fact, is possibly more susceptible to physical ills than the chemically dependent person, other than the direct toxic effect of chemicals.

Early aging occurs, for example, in the co-dependent spouse of an alcoholic who has put up with the serious drinking behavior for years and has lost all feelings of power and self-governance. Poor hygiene and grooming occur. In a more advanced stage, poor function of the different organs of the body occurs, just as it does with alcohol dependents. High blood pressure, gastritis, colitis, allergies and bronchitis are all quite common. In the female, advanced co-dependents have marked changes in their menstrual cycles and reproductive ability. Organ damage will actually occur, just as it does in chemical dependency when the disease is allowed to advance. Ulcers, heart arrhythmia, arthritis, neuritis and frequent trauma are not at all unusual as complications of advanced co-dependency.

In looking at the complications of co-dependency, the Loner goes from vague spiritual desires to suicide, the Warrior can go from family conflicts to final conflicts, and the Relic can go from early aging and hypochondria to damage of organs and death.

The actual course of the disease is not in this direction. Actually, it is just the same as it is in chemical dependency. The vague spiritual desires occur alongside family conflict and hypochondria. The loss of faith, social conflicts and poor body functions occur simultaneously. Loss of beliefs, final conflicts and damaged organs finally occur together. In essence, what we are saying is the actual course of the disease is from left to right and the stages of the severity are from top to bottom.

As their illness progresses, the conversations a co-dependent person might start holding in their head could be as follows:

**Table 13.1. Complications — The Problems**

| Spiritual Complications | Social Complications | Physical Complications |
|---|---|---|
| Self-worth struggles<br>"I'm guilty!" | Family struggles<br>"I'm unloved!" | Physical struggles<br>"I'm so tired!" |
| Higher Power disconnect<br>"I'm helpless! I'm ashamed!" | Social struggles<br>"I'm unwanted!" | Organ malfunction<br>"I'm sick!" |
| Spiritual bankruptcy<br>"I'm helpless! I'm worthless!" | Final struggles<br>"I'm unnecessary!" | Organ damage<br>"I'm dying!" |

## Post-Traumatic Stress Disorder

Tim Cermak says, "These resultant complications are not surprising either." For as we observe children from alcoholic or sexually abusive families, it becomes clear that many of their characteristics and results are the same as those seen in any individual who is suffering from the phenomenon of *Post-Traumatic Stress Disorder*. When people are subject to stresses of such intensity and nature that they clearly lie outside the range of normal human experience, they will frequently suffer from the post-traumatic stress disorder. The effects are especially severe if the stress is caused by a series of traumatic events of human origin (Cermak).

Dr. Cermak goes on to state that these effects are even more severe in those individuals who are already under stress, who have rigid coping strategies or those whose support system includes others who encourage denial of the stress. Dr. Cermak says "psychic numbing" results which at its worst leads to disassociative states, a phasing out into the ultimate denial of what is currently happening. Emotions become constricted, especially in areas where intimacy, tenderness and sexuality are involved. This lack of spontaneity and extreme control of emotions is a hallmark of co-dependents. Many also speak of how they are able to tolerate the most miserable of situations by maintaining a facade of being present and attentive in a situation, while quietly retreating to a very distant and safer place in their imaginations.

External stresses can result in many of the physical complications of co-dependency, but internal stresses that result from the continuing suppressing of feelings can result in even greater physical complications.

**Co-dependency Complications**

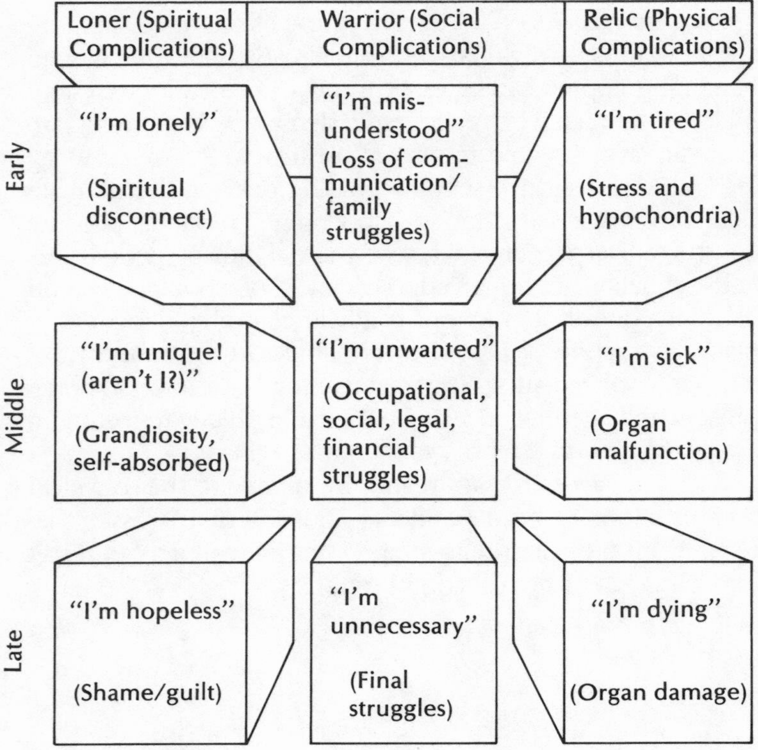


This is a summary of the ***RESULT*** of having the primary brain disease of co-dependency which is allowed to progress to secondary complications that affect the patient's ***LIFE.***

14

# Personality Dimensions And Co-dependency

## The Survival Roles And Psychiatric Disorders

Denial and delusion are necessary to explain away the craziness and dysfunction in a co-dependent's life. As individuals begin to meet their needs by using misperceptions, misconceptions, chemicals or compulsive repetitive behavior and as they integrate this into their own belief system, which has evolved from both inherited personality dimensions and their past experiences, they evolve as specific personality types.

One way to describe these personality types is to go back to Dr. C. Robert Cloniger's three dimensions of the personality of an addicted person. He found the three major dimensions of the personality used were those of *Novelty-Seeking, Harm-Avoidance* and *Reward-Dependence.* Each of these had an effect on a system within the brain, and each of them used their own set of neurotransmitters.

It is interesting to note that co-dependents who have personality testing performed will frequently show up with the following personality disorders: avoidant, dependent, obsessive/compulsive, passive/aggressive and self-defeating behavior disorder. The most common of these are the avoidant, dependent and obsessive/compulsive personality disorders. These dovetail very nicely into the same three personality dimensions of Novelty-Seeking (borderline and passive/aggressive personality disorders), Harm-Avoidance (avoidant and compulsive personality disorders) and Reward-Dependence (dependent personality disorder, self-defeating behavior disorder).

Co-dependents frequently develop the same personality dimensions (symptoms and signs) as do chemically dependent persons.

### *Novelty-Seeking*

For instance, those showing high novelty-seeking are those who are impulsive, exploratory, excitable, disorderly and distractable. If they are low novelty-seeking individuals, they will then demonstrate rigidity, reflectiveness, loyalty to a fault, orderliness and attention to details.

### *Reward-Dependence*

If their personality is one in which they are highly dependent on rewards, they will appear as one who is eager to help others, emotionally collapsed into others, warmly and energetically sympathetic, overly sentimental, sensitive and persistent, even when no results are forthcoming. If one is of lower reward dependence, they will then appear to be socially detached and cool, practical and self-willed and narcissistic and histrionic to a degree.

### *Harm-Avoidance*

Those who have high harm-avoidance demonstrate caution and apprehensiveness. They are hypervigilant, pessimistic, inhibited and shy. However, if they demonstrate low harm-avoidance, then they appear to be uncaring, uninhibited, perhaps foolish in their risk-taking, overconfident and to all outward appearance "have it all together." Individuals using these three different personality dimensions may or may not have tried alcohol and may or may not have become chemically dependent, based on how their brain responds to chemicals. But even so, behaviors can act as alcohol does on the three activation systems, with the same final common pathway in terms of disease, disorder and dysfunction.

So it appears that medicating drugs, such as alcohol and nicotine, which change the way we think and feel, and medicating behaviors, especially when they become compulsive, intense and repetitive, have similar effects and similar underpinnings.

## Survival Roles

A second approach to describing various co-dependent personality types uses the survival roles originally described by Sharon Wegscheider-Cruse in 1976 in her pamphlet, *The Family Trap.* These roles are adopted by children from dysfunctional homes such as those where a parent is addicted. The various roles are probably another way to describe manifestations of inherited personality dimensions. The symptoms (feelings) and signs (behaviors) of each of these roles are as follows:

### Family Hero

The Family Hero suffers from symptoms of pressure and responsibility, loneliness, pain, inadequacy, confusion, anger and anxiety regarding the safety of self, siblings and even parents. This is the role that Claudia Black likens to The Little Parent. The first symptoms include fear of abandonment and feeling totally responsible. The signs (behavior) of a Family

Hero are mostly obvious. They work hard for approval, they want to look good, physically and socially, appear sophisticated and grown-up, parenting the parents, striving for success and achievements. "The more I do, the less they'll fight or drink."

Family Heroes are driven by a need to be self-sufficient and independent. They do not openly ask for or accept help or counsel, but may have one or two private confidants who are the "only" ones who can understand. They have little doubt about their appointment as fixer of everything and caretaker of all. They are overly reinforced by society at very young ages. They receive praise for their mature acting-out and accomplishments. This imprint on their brain may last a lifetime. They assume and accept all the unfinished business of the parents. They frequently serve as liaison, peacemaker, clean-up person and even surrogate spouse.

In the exaggerated forms of this role, Family Heroes may be diagnosed as suffering from a Separation Anxiety Disorder or an Eating Disorder of Childhood or from Major Depressive Episodes, Generalized Anxiety Disorders, Arousal and Orgasmic Disorders and numerous other disorders of adulthood. Different degrees of Histrionic and Narcissistic Personality Disorders can be present. In the absence of such overt disorders, their co-dependency correlates best with cluster "C" of the Personality Disorders. (See Table 14.1).

**Family Scapegoat**

A second role is the Family Scapegoat, who shows symptoms of loneliness, anger, fear, hurt and of being rejected and not fitting. Their signs (behaviors) are frequently in the form of rebellion, defiance and chemical use. As children and teenagers, Scapegoats are often discipline problems, defying authority, stealing, running away from home, lying or vandalizing. On occasion, they can be cruel to their siblings, playmates or animals. They frequently draw attention to themselves and apparently feel they can get revenge if they continue "buzzing" and causing turmoil within the household. They may have explosive tempers. They often project onto others problems that arise from their own mistakes. They have a great deal of distrust, resentment and vindictiveness about them. They place great emphasis and value on peers, usually peers who are also scapegoats.

In its exaggerated form, the Scapegoat role may be diagnosed as a Conduct Disorder or Oppositional Defiant Disorder of Childhood, or Depressive Adjustment, Impulse Control Disorders of Adolescence and Early Adulthood. Most of the time the Scapegoat's co-dependency only evolves into a cluster of symptoms and signs as seen in cluster "C" of the Personality Disorders. (See Table 14.1).

**Lost Child**

The Lost Child is one who learns not to make connections and not to make waves. The symptoms (feelings) of inadequacy, loss, disillusionment and fear of conflict and loneliness cover up a boiling cauldron of anger. Their behavior (signs) are those of quietness and distancing, sometimes being overweight, being aloof, avoiding all but those whom they know quite well, mostly family members and very close peers or familiar figures. This behavior can begin as early as two and a half years of age. Although they may have difficulty in school, they may be considered the best behaved at home.

These individuals are easily hurt by criticism or disapproval, and they want guarantees that they will be liked before they establish any kind of relationship with someone. They are also quite reticent in groups and fear being embarrassed. They exaggerate the difficulties of tasks because they do not want to fail. They actually will avoid tasks to their own detriment. They may cancel social plans because they feel they would become too exhausted from the effort of getting ready for such an event. They are unwilling to take on jobs or positions that might require social contacts.

In its most exaggerated forms the Lost Child may be diagnosed as an Avoidant Disorder and Eating Disorder or

**Table. 14.1. Correlation of exaggerated CoA survival roles & DSM III-R Criteria for Mental Disorders**

| Family Hero | Scapegoat | Lost Child | Mascot | Chemically Dependent Chief Enabler Or Any Of The Other Survival Roles |
|---|---|---|---|---|
| **Disorders First Evident In Infancy, Childhood Or Adolescence** | | | | |
| Separation anxiety disorder (309.21)<br>Eating disorders (307.X) | Conduct disorder group type (312.20)<br>Oppositional defiant disorder (313.81) | Avoidant disorder of childhood (313.21)<br>Academic skills disorder (315.XX)<br>Eating disorder (307.XX) | Attention deficit hyperactivity disorder (314.01)<br>Overanxious disorder (313.00) | Separation anxiety disorder (309.21)<br>Overanxious disorder (313.00)<br>Eating disorders (307.X)<br>Identity disorder (313.82) |
| **Psycho-active Substance Use Disorders, Mood Disorders, Anxiety Disorders, Sexual Disorders, Body Disorders** | | | | |
| Major depressive episodes, recurrent (296.3X)<br>Generalized anxiety disorder hypervigilant (300.02)<br>Arousal and orgasmic disorders (302.2 & 302.7X) | Depressive disorder (311.00) NOS*<br>Manic-depressive moderately severe cyclothymia (300.13)<br>Adjustment disorder disturbed conduct (309.30) recurrent | Chronic depressive dysthymia (300.4)<br>Low sexual desire disorder (302.XX)<br>Adjustment disorder with depressed mood and with physical complaints (309.00 & 309.82) recurrent | Manic-depressive moderately severe cyclothymic (301.13)<br>Adjustment disorder, disturbed emotions and conduct (309.40) recurrent | Psycho-active substance dependence (alcohol, 303.90 — other, 304.XX)<br>Depressive episodes, NOS* or secondary dysthymia (311.0 or 300.40)<br>Post-traumatic stress disorder (309.89) |

| **Psycho-active Substance Use Disorders, Mood Disorders, Anxiety Disorders, Sexual Disorders, Body Disorders (cont'd)** | | | | |
|---|---|---|---|---|
| Adjustment disorder with anxious mood (309.24) recurrent<br>Obsessive/compulsive neuroses (300.3) (300.3 & 301.6)<br>Body dysmorphic disorder (abnormal body image) (300.70) | Impulse control disorder, explosive (312.34) | Hypochondriasis (300.7) | | Sexual disorder repeated conquests (302.90 - 2)<br>*NOS - not otherwise specified |
| **Personality Disorders, Self-defeating Behaviors** | | | | |
| Histrionic personality disorder (301.50)<br>Narcissistic pers. disorder (301.81)<br>Obsessive/compulsive personality disorder (301.6) | Paranoid personality disorder (301.00)<br>Anti-social personality disorder (301.7)<br>Borderline personality disorder (301.83) | Schizoid personality disorder (301.2) | Borderline personality disorder (301.83) | Cluster "C" Personality Disorders<br>1. Avoidant (301.82)<br>2. Dependent (301.60)<br>3. Obsessive/compulsive (301.40)<br>4. Passive/aggressive (301.84)<br>Self-defeating personality disorder (XXX.XX) |

From: Painful Affairs: Looking For Love Through Addiction And Co-Dependency by Joseph R. Cruse, M.D. ©1989

Academic Skills Disorder of Childhood. They tend to receive medication for long-standing depressions. There are associated or primary Adjustment Disorders and physical complaints and Sexual Desire Disorders (Diminished). They may dissociate so far from reality into their own world that they develop a Schizoid Personality Disorder of Adulthood. (See Table 14.1).

The Lost Child and the Scapegoat, struggling to belong and to be liked, are high risks for chemical dependency and pregnancy out of wedlock. Many never feel they belong, no matter what their sacrifice. Suicide, for the teen or the adult Lost Child or Scapegoat is sometimes the final sacrifice. When their symptoms are less than this, their co-dependency correlates best with cluster "C" of the Personality Disorders. (See Table 14.1).

**Family Mascot**

The final role is the Family Mascot. This is a child whose symptoms (feelings) are fear, insecurity, low self-worth, loneliness and anxiety. The Mascot acts out (signs) just the opposite, using any strategy or play to attract attention. Being the family clown, being hyperactive and moving with short bursts of energy seem to be their assignments in the family. They often fidget or squirm, unable to remain in their seat. They cannot follow through on instructions. They have difficulty staying with one activity until it's completed. They are often quite noisy, talkative and interrupt others. They lose things and frequently engage in distractions that do not go along with the crowd. They blurt out questions without thinking and answer before the question is completed. Often they have difficulty taking a turn or waiting in line.

In its exaggerated forms the Mascot may be diagnosed as an Attention Deficit/Hyperactivity Disorder or Over-Anxious Disorder of Childhood. As adults to young adults they may be treated for manic-depressive behaviors of varying severity. They continue to suffer from an Adjustment Disorder of mostly the Disturbed Emotions and Conduct Type. They can evolve into a Borderline Personality Disorder. Less than this, their co-dependency correlates best with cluster "C" of the Personality Disorders.

It is important to realize that these roles are not rigid, that they are frequently interchanged and combined. Children may assume certain characteristics of one role at a stage of their life and then assume characteristics of several roles at some other stage. These are enduring traits, however, that are somewhat pervasive and permanent. Pervasive means that these traits affect most things we do and feel. Permanent means they are probably with us for life. This is not all bad and in some ways is good as our structure of traits is part of our personality. However, when traits become exaggerated into a disorder, the disorder is not necessarily permanent and may respond to treatment. A disorder results when one or more of our traits become so exaggerated that it interferes with our lives and causes us ongoing, severe emotional pain.

Again, we have a person who, because of compulsions and the need to medicate, has affected their brain and their ability to function so greatly that they lose their choices of freedom, behavior and thinking. They lose more than just choices — they lose some memory and they lose the ability to predict on any given occasion just how they will feel, what they will think or how they will behave. Their reactions are so variable, their feelings so inconsistent, and their actions so impulsive, that they cannot on any given occasion claim to be predictable or even dependable — not unlike an alcoholic.

Co-dependency, like addiction, is a chronic, progressive and ultimately fatal disease if not treated. Also, like addiction, it can be successfully treated. Increased understanding of its signs, symptoms, complications and its relationship to personality disorders and dimensions all contribute to successful treatment and recovery.

# Summary To Part II

The Signs and Symptoms of a disease describe that disease as it affects an individual.

*Symptoms* are those events experienced by the individual themselves. In co-dependency, most of those symptoms are the *emotions* and beliefs that the individual experiences.

*Signs* are those events in a disease that can be observed by an outside observer as well as the co-dependent individual. Signs are usually *behaviors* and thought processes that the individual exhibits.

In co-dependency, signs and symptoms can be grouped into three major divisions of signs and symptoms that describe how it affects the individuals *brain:*

- Delusion/Denial (The Deluded Lover)
- Suppression (Behavioral Medicator)
- Compulsions (Overdoer)

Complications of a disease are those events that occur as a result of the progression of the untreated disease and describe how that disease affects the individual's *life.*

In co-dependency most of the complications can be grouped into three major divisions which closely parallel the complications of chemical dependency. They are:

- Low Self-Worth (Spiritual Complications)
- Interpersonal Problems (Social Complications)
- Medical Problems (Physical Complications)

EPILOGUE

# My Co-dependency Story

This story might be entitled a "Tragedy of Errors" which later turns into a "Conspiracy of Silence." The errors were mainly in perception on the part of a young boy and then later in a young man trying to figure it out. I was positive I was right.

I watched my father and I remember how everyone seemed to love Dad in the town of 2,000 where we lived. He was what everyone would consider successful. I deduced that being loved was what led to wealth (which I thought we had — again a misperception), which led to excitement, attention and even power. For some compelling reason, I loved each of those qualities and wanted to attain them for myself. I decided I would go for it. I wanted all five, actually, in spades — excitement, attention, power, wealth, success.

As I began my campaign even as a young boy, I found that pretending and not letting anyone find out what I didn't know or what my motives really were required constant vigilance. My trial-and-error attempts were productive more often than not. I valued my successful attempts, and covered up my unsuccessful attempts, perhaps even more than the usual youngster would do.

## Secrets

I became so proficient at covering up, that the process of covering up and not being discovered was itself a source of excitement for me. I loved the feeling. I had secrets. I loved almost everything I did. I was excited by almost everything I did. I knew I was phony, but I could cover that up. I also knew I was "chicken" and that required hypervigilance on a daily basis to avoid what I feared most, the unmerciful beating that all chickens get eventually just because they are chickens. I was not found out. I covered that up at least to when my drinking began.

I decided that women were very special creatures, delicate and desirable, and that they required special care. I loved them. Anything that a woman would let me do, I considered a great favor. I never would be good enough, really, but if I could capture a beautiful and sensuous woman, as my dad had done, then people would really believe that I was good enough.

My greatest secret was that I was put on earth for a purpose, a special purpose, maybe even by God. I felt that I was different, special, but I also knew that I had better not be found out having such thoughts or people would call me crazy or worst of all, conceited.

They called me my father's son, including my love for drink. Already at a young age, I was losing my zest and tiring, but I looked like him, I walked like him, I made sure that I acted like him. I was becoming worn-out at an early age.

## Headworld

It is hard to say just when the child who I was went into his own head and began to live in that isolated "headworld" for the next 40-plus years of his life. Some people seem to relate to a time in their childhood when all their feelings shut down, thus marking the death of their inner child. As a young child I was in awe of the world around me. I was full of energy, trust, excitement, insight and unconditional love.

I know now that my feeling child has not been alive for every year I have been on this earth. Most of my life has been lived in a world separate and apart. That world is what I call my "headworld." Apparently things were too mysterious and too fast for me, no one was explaining them to me. There was no way for me to learn except from my immediate environment, from the events that were occurring and even more so from those events that were not occurring except in my imagination. So I drew my own conclusions.

I concluded that the only safe place for me was with adults, that if I strayed off alone, I would be lost, swallowed up or set upon. I had the feeling that the adults around me did not notice me much and that if they didn't notice me, they might forget me. I strove to prevent that from happening. There were times when I felt shut out. There were times when I was told to shut up so there was a lot of my young life where I shut up and shut down. I was an expert at pouting, I could sit around on the other side of the garage all day and pout.

## Selective Hearing

I knew there were answers. I also knew there were special answers for me and that it was up to me to figure out those answers. It didn't take long for me to stop listening even when they did talk to me. I began selective hearing. People were going to have to tell me: "You are fantastic! We notice you and because of that you are worthwhile."

I began my observations, my deductions, my "childlike" logic and my conclusions. My first conclusion was that the Cruse family was special, that Bert Cruse, Father, was "king," and that Mother would take care of us and keep us safe. Nothing was actually said along those lines, but it was implicitly ingrained in me and, as I later found out, my brothers and sisters as well. We did not talk to one another. It was almost as if we didn't have to . . . we knew.

I had no doubt that our family was a combination of *My Three Sons* and *Ozzie and Harriet.* I also wanted to identify with the *Andy Hardy* movies I saw when I was growing up.

When Andy was stressed, worried or misbehaving, he was lovingly taken into his father's study. His father was a judge, and the study was all books and leather and wisdom. His father shared that wisdom with Andy. I envied that. I gathered up books and sat among them playing the wise father, paying attention to his son whom he loved so much.

*Pepper Young*, a radio soap opera character, learned early on how to live an adult life. I knew I needed to grow up and be just like him and that I had lots of learning to do very fast.

The Barber family, who were on the radio in the '30s and '40s, had dinner every Sunday at Papa Barber's house. I not only felt that my father was Papa Barber, but that I had to do everything possible to grow up just like Papa Barber and have Sunday dinner with my spouse, children and grandchildren present each and every Sunday. That's the way it's done! I dreamed of doing that for years.

All of my knowledge was based on my observations of one family, just ours. Other homes I went into as a child were simply copies of my own family. I did not see any differences through my child's eyes. I perceived reality and normality as it was in our family. I began to pretend and later believe that I had significant power and that I would gain my parents' love and respect and the love and respect of the world if they would only just notice. Obviously this need to be noticed was manifest by behavior that today would probably be called hyperactive or manic. My "headworld" fantasies had my parents loving me the perfect way I had to be loved. Any helplessness that I felt, I fantasized into strength. Minor accomplishments were blown up into the myth of "mission accomplished." I had succeeded.

## Relationships

I carried the same behaviors into adulthood. I would go to any lengths to be noticed and liked. I fully fantasized that I had the power to make someone love me, and I was quite creative and innovative in getting that job done. I was able to be charming, grandiose, convincing, needy and persuasive to get my way with members of the opposite sex in high school and into young adulthood. My pattern of emotional immaturity was repeated over and over again.

As far as my relationships with males were concerned, those that were non-threatening to me — and they were in the minority — saw me as a self-restricting and avoiding character. Which in their words would have come out as "chicken" and "stuck-up." My fears of being abandoned and of being "less than" or not measuring up were soon joined by fears of discovery and its ultimate punishment, physical beatings by the "big guys."

My behavior can be summarized as follows. During my childhood I was always in the way. During my adolescence I was most comfortable when noticed by those who were smart or had the most money or were the best athletes and yet weren't tough guys. In high school athletics made us macho, and I thought I would be noticed. So go for the letter sweater!

**Sports Hero**

I was raised by a father who was from a small farm and who was never involved in sports except to watch an occasional baseball game. Throughout my adolescent and high school years sports were an extremely important status symbol. I was completely perplexed and could not understand Dad's minimal interest in my football, basketball and baseball strivings. Physically I was thin and had red curly hair. Constitutionally I was scared to death. But my motivation to be accepted and obtain some kind of concrete evidence of my worth drove me to participate day after day in sports. I endured grueling practices and weekly despair sitting on the bench, hoping and fearing I'd be put into the game.

Two vivid memories exemplify my motivation for participating in sports. One was the sudden appearance of my father at the last of my Pony League baseball games. It was the ninth inning with two outs. We were losing badly. I was put into the game to pinch-hit and got a walk. While standing on first base, I saw my father's face in the crowd, and I immediately broke for second without any knowledge of where the ball was. It happened to be in the pitcher's hand. It quickly went to the second baseman's hand, and I ended the season for our team, striving to be noticed.

Another occasion was in a huge old baseball park in Denver, where four Little League football games were going on at the same time. On one of my rare occasions of being put into the game, I made a downfield tackle by myself. I immediately stood up, shielding my eyes, looking for my father in the stands. There must have been five to six thousand people there. I stood there until the coach had to take me off the field, while I searched the crowd for his face.

I chose to participate in sports because they were macho, even though my father had no interest in them. I went out for them for what it was worth, playing football almost suicidally as a tall, skinny senior who could hardly make a team in a small town. I decided as a parent that I would always be there for my sons' sports activities, but I realized later that I actually used my sons for my second chance to relive my athletic career. I pressured my children to be there for me and my purposes.

I tried class plays, class offices, student council offices, volunteer work, church work, debating in school, spelling bees and even substituting for the local minister on two occasions during his summer vacation. I made up the sermons at the last minute and received congratulations afterwards, thinking, "I put it over on them." (However, I felt some measure of comfort and familiarity in that role. Strange.)

### Doctor Hero

One of my greatest affirmations as a youngster came when I was five or six. I declared that I wanted to be a "doctor." My sister had typhoid fever and the local family practitioner came every day to give us all shots of gamma globulin, the only possible preventive medicine at that time. She almost died. But he was able to tend to her and pull her through. She was hospitalized in our small mining town where they had only a 12-bed hospital. Each day when he would come,

I would hate the shot but was fascinated by the smell of his bag and made my declaration that I wanted to grow up and become a doctor. It was more than just the smell of the bag. I saw how he was received in our home and how he was talked about after he left and how important he was to our family and my sister. I liked the aura about him and I wanted that. The reinforcement validation came with my declaration.

Dr. Joe Pursch describes the little boy who runs into the house and says, "Mommy, Mommy, I want to be a race car driver," and the reply is, "Yes, honey, go wash up for supper." Later, the little boy runs into the house and says, "Mommy, Mommy, I want to be a fireman," and the reply is "Yes, honey, get ready for bed." Later the little boy says, "Mommy, I want to be a doctor" . . . and *the whole western world comes to a screeching stop!* Mommy says, "Grandma, come listen to what Johnny said. He wants to grow up and be a doctor!"

## Hero Worship

Like that little boy, I received validation all through my growing years just because I chose that profession. I learned the process of living vicariously through other people, and not all of them were heroes. Some of them were not in my best interest. Most of them were not even aware I was using them. I was not even aware I was using them. I know now that hero worship has consumed much of my life.

I went to the university with Second World War veterans who were mature, married and had children, and who actually talked back to the professors. I was more occupied with their noticing me and respecting me, than I was with what I was supposed to be learning in class. I was also totally preoccupied with what was happening back home with my high school girlfriend and whether or not she cared for me, even though I was at a distance while attending the university. I failed to develop peer friendships, being unable to stay in a fraternity of individuals my own age, but would rather chum around with my brother and his friends, who were four years older. I was their freshman mascot.

I worked as an orderly, taking twice as long to accomplish simple tasks, so that they would be done perfectly. I rode the bus 200 miles home as many times a month as I possibly could, seeking to re-establish those "good ole days" in high school, especially as far as my high school romance was concerned.

The pilgrimages back to the small town of my high school days continued both mentally and emotionally for the next 35 years. Then the town suddenly stepped out of its myth and I became aware that it had nothing further to offer me. For many years I was worthwhile, not because I was, but because I came from that small Colorado mountain town.

In college my progressing disease of co-dependency had many of the aspects of the compulsive, obsessed lover who was in delusion and who continued to medicate with higher and more intense doses of behavior and accomplishment and whose reality, insight and intellect suffered. In fact, I was well into the complication phases of my co-dependency, that of spiritual complications and relationship complications, when "I found it" . . . alcohol.

## Alcohol

Alcohol provided a 25-year masking of my progressing co-dependency. From the age of 18 to 20 until I was 43 years old, alcohol was my chief medicator. Nicotine was its assistant, providing a good booster and good maintenance during the times I was without alcohol. You see, alcohol worked for me because I was programmed for it by the genes I inherited from my parents and maybe their parents. My inherited and acquired personality dimensions of Harm-Avoidance, Reward-Dependence and Novelty-Seeking similarly allowed my co-dependence to flourish simultaneously.

As I grew older my behaviors, especially those that dealt with control, attention, prestige, power-seeking and grandiosity, began to pay off and give me those "rushes" that I desperately needed. I became obsessed in my thoughts and compulsive in my behaviors. I was like the young lover who has found *the one* who would give him whatever he wanted and needed.

It was hard work and I had to continually try to remedy errors and model myself after those who seemed successful. At the same time my head was buzzing with new ways of figuring it out and getting it. As I found behaviors that resulted in successful rushes, I discovered they did indeed medicate and for a time calm the pain and fear, only to have pain and fear re-emerge. I now was medicating with frenetic behavior at an increasing rate as my tolerance to novelty developed and my fears outdid my rushes. I had to increase the intensity, the frequency and the duration of my compulsions, my delusions and my frenetic desperate medicators. More alcohol, work, accomplishments, notoriety, sex, spending and controlling kept the rush going.

## Denial Behaviors

My denial, my misinformation, my low self-worth and my medicating behaviors were there even after I stopped drinking. I used extramarital enmeshments, professional success, excitement, crisis and nicotine for my medicators. Within my own home, I tried to control, control, control. By drinking, the discomforts and the pain that might have normally intervened and motivated me to seek a healthy nondependent way of life were medicated and no longer available to me. My disease of alcoholism provided a 25-year delaying action.

The delay is even longer than 25 years when the first eight years of my sobriety are added. Eight years during which I was just lonely and yearning, trying and failing, but at least abstinent from alcohol. My major sense of self-worth was that I was a recovering alcoholic.

## Co-dependent Denial

During those eight years, I led a double life. One life was as an active, recovering member of a 12-Step recovery program. The other was as a struggling, unhappy member of a coupleship and a family whose various levels of co-dependency continued to go unnoticed and untreated. We did not know there was help available. We did not know that we needed help. We did not know that anything was wrong now that the drinking was over. I knew there was a lack of intimacy, both emotional and sexual, in our coupleship. There was also a lack of intimacy, trust, awareness and teaching in the family. We all cared desperately for each other, we were all proud of each other and we all asked each other how we felt on a daily basis, but nobody answered, really. Perhaps they did answer but were unheard.

Then programs for family members of alcoholics began to emerge, but since I was already sober, we didn't consider them necessary for us. And the troubles continued, especially for our now spiritually dead coupleship. Suddenly the realization that sobriety doesn't fix everything hit me. We began personal involvement in several straightforward outpatient family programs dealing with family negotiations subsequent to recovery from alcoholism. Individual denial, compulsion and suppression of feelings was not dealt with. Low self-worth, intimacy and relationship problems were not addressed. Insight and acceptance improved a bit. Each family member's co-dependency escaped almost unscathed. Our pain renewed. Each of us continued our own self-styled survival plans, drawing our own conclusions about the usefulness of life and the future.

The concept of co-dependency began to emerge. It was difficult for me to understand and more difficult for me to believe it was "scientifically" valid. But most sadly, I could not apply it to me or members of my family. It was my contention that my family members were all very normal and unaffected persons who each simply had some troubles, rather than persons afflicted with co-dependency.

### Life Changes

Then three events occurred:

First, after 31 years of marriage, in which the last 13 were spiritually dead as far as a coupleship was concerned, I again asked "Will I ever have a chance with you?" The answer again was, "I doubt it." I acted on the answer, and even though I still didn't believe it, I left. I have never returned.

However, I only left physically. For the next year and a half, I remained emotionally and dependently connected through hours of counseling and control games and hope.

Second, after 22 years of practicing obstetrics and gynecology, I changed careers into the field of addictionology. I had a golden opportunity to be involved in the development of a great treatment center and then became involved in the operation of that center.

Third, I began my recovery from my co-dependency. Recovery didn't occur overnight, but it occurred fast enough and soon enough to save me from spiritual, personal and professional disaster and from eventually succumbing to one or both of my diseases. The timing is similar to the timely intervention into my chemical dependency. I consider these Divine Timings.

**Choices**

I began to learn about co-dependency, especially our pathological dependency on others. I began to feel a sense of value and worth about myself as I set up housekeeping, began to make my own choices and to sort out my two lives. I took my own power and found the joy of being 100 percent responsible for myself. I probably began to appear self-centered to others as I learned how to be the centered self I had always longed to be.

I began by leaving a marriage, getting a divorce and disengaging from a dependency on the same person that began when I was 12 years old. My dependency had continued through our marriage, which began when I was 19 and she was 18 and continued for 34 years. I have prayed that my own relief and sense of freedom from the dependency that these two teenagers had endured through the years has happened for her as well.

There have been many people throughout my life who seemed to see a spiritual and "good" part of me that I was unable to acknowledge. They wished the best for me, but were not given permission by me to help or come close to me. It seems that those who loved me most, I took for granted. Those who were unattainable or unreachable were the focus of my energies. I believed the put downs and criticisms from those unreachable ones . . . and vowed to do better.

It is now apparent that enough of my true spiritual and independent self began to evolve early in my recovery from co-dependency so that Sharon, my present wife, was attracted to me. She made it clear she could see my spiritual good . . . and for the first time I did not feel as though I had misled someone again. I began to believe she was right about me. So rather than take her for granted as I had done the others, I took her seriously and began to accept her love and love her in kind. I hadn't known how to do this before. I found freedom in my unconditional commitment to her. I found more self-worth in her commitment to me.

At last! The game playing was over! A spade was a spade! I believed and was believed. All secrets were disclosed. And since much of my sickness reflected in my secrets, even from childhood, I got better. Life got easier . . . but not all at once.

Hundreds of thousands of words passed between us. Many thousands of them were painful words. Concepts, beliefs, needs and wants and boundaries were laid out in the open. We needed help. We found John, a therapist.

My continuing belief in tradition and my dedication to my dream of the perfect father and head of a perfect family stood as a great impediment to my total freedom to choose and build a new relationship. I didn't trust psychotherapy, couple counseling or even John at first. After I trusted all three, I still didn't want to give up my paternal dream. I suffered, as many co-dependent people suffer, from what I call "The Cake and Eat It Too Syndrome."

**Boundaries**

Boundary setting is absolutely necessary for recovery. There is a fallout of pain and confusion in others when boundaries are set. Fear causes me to overstate or to understate my boundaries when I see anger, confusion and disagreement arising in others. I've had to hold fast and hold faith that understanding will arise from misunderstanding. I have had to protect my recovery from perplexed, angry and doubting family members and friends.

We have had to protect the priorities of our coupleship on blind faith, from outside invaders, such as families, careers, pressures, prestige-producing activities and so forth. My dependency on persons, places, and things is not entirely gone.

Boundaries and priorities still require daily attention. Some, however, are permanently set and the benefits are accruing. Some examples:

| | |
|---|---|
| *To my wife:* | Our coupleship comes only after my personal recovery programs and my Higher Power. |
| *To myself:* | My parenting days are over. I will always be a father, but in title only, not in an active role. |
| *To old friends:* | Love me, love Sharon, love us and my love is there for you. |
| *To new friends:* | My investments in nurturing of others require reciprocal investment and nurturing for me. |
| *To my employees and colleagues:* | Mutual respect, cooperation and gratitude will sustain our relationships. |
| *To my children:* | I pray for a loving and close adult/adult relationship with my adult children. Their chosen coupleships are twosomes and are inviolate, as is mine. |

Honestly, I cannot speak for any other member of my family. I have not lived in their skin. I have seen their pain, felt their anger and confusion, and I have been as perplexed as they. We have all probably felt stepped on and invalidated from time to time. My adult children need to be free. If they demand their freedom from me, they have it. I love my daughter and my sons and I hope they love me. What we need now from each other are continued expressions of caring, love and support and expressed gratitude that we had the opportunities to live, love and grow together.

## Freedom And Challenge

In addition to setting boundaries, my recovery has required that I make additional choices. My spirit is such that I must be free to create and innovate. I am not destined for a singular lifetime career, especially in detailed administration, routine and repetition. Once the two years of designing and creating the chemical dependency recovery hospital were over and after two additional years of involvement in administering its programs, it became apparent to all that I could no longer serve it or myself well. I was making major changes in my personal life, recovering my creative self and therefore needed to be free to move on. I left the Betty Ford Center.

Betty Ford gently described what she saw in me in her book, *Betty — A Glad Awakening.*

***"We regretted his leaving, but Joe is a visionary, he is always searching for the next challenge."***

In addition to searching for the next challenge, I was also searching for the next step in my recovery from co-dependency and chemical dependency. And there it was!

## Nicotine Withdrawal

In 10 years of abstaining from the mind-altering effects of alcohol and pills, I was *still* actively addicted to the reinforcing and mind-altering effects of nicotine. I began a three-month struggle of detoxing on my own and finally became abstinent and physically detoxed in a seven-day period. My psychological dependence required daily attention ("I don't smoke," I told myself with every urge) for the next three months. I had used alcohol and pills as medicators and was still medicated by cigarettes. I didn't realize how much until the cigarettes were gone.

Simultaneously with giving up cigarettes, I was surrendering my life-long myth of the perfect family. "Papa Barber" would not be seeing the kids and grandkids every Sunday for dinner. At that stage and under the strained conditions of my new recovery, Papa Barber realized he might never see his kids or grandkids again! The myth went and the grief set in.

A dream formulated by a little kid and sustained in unreality by a co-dependent adult had to die. With death there is mourning, and for the first year that I was free of nicotine and I had my feelings completely available to me, I cried. I cried on the steering wheel of my car a lot. I cried at the sight of grandpas and their grandkids. I cried after difficult phone calls. I cried when an airliner passed over my former home town at 33,000 feet. I clung to memories and I cried and I clung and I cried. The feelings finally escaped, and under the sadness and grief there was anger. It came roaring up like vomitus.

## Discharge

Anger on behalf of a kid raised in a silent, shut-down family. Silent violence. Anger at my own cowardice and fear. Anger at heroes, including women, who fell from their pedestals. Anger at power-mongers who stifled me and yet whom I held in awe. Anger at others' lack of understanding regarding my attempts to recover, renew and finally re-order my life. A great relief and sense of worth came over me as I discharged that anger therapeutically. At that moment I no longer felt like a gutted deer.

These events all occurred at times of physical, personal and professional crises and required the extensive use of John, perseverence on my part and the unending support, patience and understanding of Sharon. We now reap the benefits of our efforts.

After surrendering the cigarettes and the myths, and after discharging the feelings, healing began. With healing came behavior change. I lowered my expectations of people and events to a level that assured me safety and serenity.

I gave up heroes. I divorced them. I realized that I am not special because of them. They are there. We do not make or improve upon each other. I am now happily abstaining from hero worship. Although I occasionally slip and make a high school athlete or an Olympic skier or diver a hero, he or she does not influence my sense of well-being or worth. I no longer wish to be anything, be anywhere, be with anyone other than who I am and where I am, with Sharon at this moment.

### My New Love

I am not dependent on Sharon nor she on me. Each of us can live without the other. Losing her would be agonizing, but I could and would go on and could and would be happy. She is the same regarding me. At one time in my life, I felt as though I couldn't live (and I tried not to by attempting suicide) without the love of the one person I had decided God put on earth for me. What grandiosity! What a burden for that person.

Now Sharon and I choose to be with each other on a daily basis. The result is a sense of exciting freedom and joy. We have 100 percent responsibility for ourselves, all of us. If we are in a committed coupleship or alone, we must assume the responsibility for being there.

### My New Life

I have become my own hero and own best friend. This has led me to a new career, new friends, a serenity and a satisfaction with the job of living well each day. There will always be room for improvement in the days to come.

My fears are dissipating. Many of my current male friends are macho and tough and have been through a lot themselves. They are also huggers and best of all they say to me . . . "Luv ya, Big Guy!"

And what of my learnings and yearnings? Am I still alone and waiting? My learnings have been thus: My recovery is an active program, my recovery program is a solo job. My waiting is still a waiting, not in sorrow and loneliness, but in anticipation of what my Higher Power may have in store for me. I am not waiting for something to happen. I have no doubt that some things will happen, both positive and negative.

I am grateful to be well and into my learnings, and a major learning is perhaps about my yearnings. My yearnings are my driving force now. My yearnings are a challenge, not a deficit, not a burden, not daydreaming, not a cause for scorn. In the past I was told I would never be satisfied, never be happy, because I was always yearning . . . now I know that isn't true. My spiritual hunger and hunger for love and connection are being satisfied one day at a time.

Meanwhile, my yearnings remain my driving force, my excitement, my celebration! My yearnings determine my future as I respond to them . . . I have learned that I cannot but respond to them . . . for my yearnings are my essence . . .

# BIBLIOGRAPHY


Ackerman, Robert, Ph.D., "New Perspectives on Adult Children of Alcoholics," *E.A.P. Digest*, Jan/Feb, 1987.

Anonymous, **Alcoholics Anonymous**, Alcoholics Anonymous World Service, New York City, 3rd Edition.

Bergland, Richard, **The Fabric of the Mind**, Viking Press, New York & London, 1986.

Bly, Robert, **Leaping Poetry, An Idea with Poems and Translations**, Bereau Press, Boston, 1973.

Brown, Stephanie, **Treating Adult Children of Alcoholics**, John Wiley, New York, New York, 1988.

Cermak, Timmen L., **Diagnosing and Treating Co-dependency**, Johnson Institute, Minneapolis, Minnesota, 1986.

Cloninger, C. Robert, "A Systematic Method for Clinical Description and Classification of Personality Variants," *Practical General Psychology*, Vol. 44, June, 1987.

Cloninger, C. Robert, "Neurogenetic Adaptive Mechanisms in Alcoholism," *Science*, Vol. 236, April 24, 1987.

Cocores, James A., M.D., "Co-Addiction: A Silent Epidemic," *Psychiatry Letter*, Fair Oaks Hospital, Summit, New Jersey, February, 1987.

Cohen, Sidney, **The Chemical Brain, The Neurochemistry of Addictive Disorders**, Care Institute, Minneapolis, Minnesota, 1988.

**Diagnostic and Statistical Manual of Nervous and Mental Disorders**, Revised Third Edition, Washington, D.C., American Psychiatric Association, 1987.

Ford, Betty, With Chris Chase, **A Glad Awakening**, Doubleday, Garden City, New York, 1987.

Gold, Mark, **The Good News About Depression**, Villard Books, New York, New York, 1987.

Gonella, Joseph S., "Staging of Disease," *Journal of the American Medical Association,* February 3, 1984, Vol. 251, No. 5.

Jellinek, E.M., **The Disease Concept of Alcoholism**, College and University Press, New Haven, Connecticut, 1960.

Jung, Carl, In "Letters to Bill W.," *The Grapevine,* World Service, New York, New York.

McAuliffe, Robert and Mary, **Essentials for the Diagnosis of Chemical Dependency**, American Chemical Dependency Society, Minneapolis, Minnesota, 1975.

McLain, Paul, Quoted by Richard M. Restak in **The Brain: The Last Frontier.**

Mohler, Henry K., "The Intoxications" in **Handbook of Medical Treatment,** ed. by John C. DeCosta Jr., M.D., Vol. One, F.A. Davis, Philadelphia, 1919.

Restak, Richard M., **The Brain: The Last Frontier**, Doubleday, New York, 1979.

Subby, Robert, **Lost in the Shuffle: The Co-dependent Reality**, Health Communications, Pompano Beach, Florida, 1987.

Valles, Jorge, **From Social Drinking to Alcoholism**, Tane Press, Dallas, Texas, 1972.

Wegscheider-Cruse, Sharon, **Family Trap**, Nurturing Networks, Rapid City, South Dakota, 1976.

Wegscheider-Cruse, Sharon, **Choicemaking: For Co-dependents, Adult Children, and Spirituality Seekers**, Health Communications, Pompano Beach, Florida, 1985.

Wegscheider-Cruse, Sharon, **The Co-dependency Trap**, Nurturing Networks, Rapid City, South Dakota, 1988.

Whitfield, Charles L., **Healing the Child Within: Discovery and Recovery for Adult Children of Dysfunctional Families,** Health Communications, Pompano Beach, Florida, 1987.

Wilson, William, **The Best of Bill,** AA Grapevine, Inc., New York, New York, 1958.

# *Books from . . .*<br>*Health Communications*

*AFTER THE TEARS: Reclaiming The Personal Losses of Childhood*
Jane Middelton-Moz and Lorie Dwinnel
Your lost childhood must be grieved in order for you to recapture your self-worth and enjoyment of life. This book will show you how.
**ISBN 0-932194-36-2** **$7.95**

*HEALING YOUR SEXUAL SELF*
Janet Woititz
How can you break through the aftermath of sexual abuse and enter into healthy relationships? Survivors are shown how to recognize the problem and deal effectively with it.
**ISBN 1-55874-018-X** **$7.95**

*RECOVERY FROM RESCUING*
Jacqueline Castine
Effective psychological and spiritual principles teach you when to take charge, when to let go, and how to break the cycle of guilt and fear that keeps you in the responsibility trap. Mind-altering ideas and exercises will guide you to a more carefree life.
**ISBN 1-55874-016-3** **$7.95**

*ADDICTIVE RELATIONSHIPS: Reclaiming Your Boundaries*
Joy Miller
We have given ourselves away to spouse, lover, children, friends or parents. By examining where we are, where we want to go and how to get there, we can reclaim our personal boundaries and the true love of ourselves.
**ISBN 1-55874-003-1** **$7.95**

*RECOVERY FROM CO-DEPENDENCY:*
*It's Never Too Late To Reclaim Your Childhood*
Laurie Weiss, Jonathan B. Weiss
Having been brought up with life-repressing decisions, the adult child recognizes something isn't working. This book shows how to change decisions and live differently and fully.
**ISBN 0-932194-85-0** **$9.95**

---

Orders must be prepaid by check, money order, MasterCard or Visa. Purchase orders from agencies accepted (attach P.O. documentation) for billing. Net 30 days.

Minimum shipping/handling — $1.25 for orders less than $25. For orders over $25, add 5% of total for shipping and handling. Florida residents add 6% sales tax.

Enterprise Center, 3201 S.W. 15th Street,
Deerfield Beach, FL 33442
1-800-851-9100

# *Other Books By . . .*
# *Health Communications, Inc.*

*ADULT CHILDREN OF ALCOHOLICS*
Janet Woititz
Over a year on *The New York Times* Best-Seller list, this book is the primer on Adult Children of Alcoholics.
**ISBN 0-932194-15-X** **$6.95**

*STRUGGLE FOR INTIMACY*
Janet Woititz
Another best-seller, this book gives insightful advice on learning to love more fully.
**ISBN 0-932194-25-7** **$6.95**

*DAILY AFFIRMATIONS: For Adult Children of Alcoholics*
Rokelle Lerner
These positive affirmations for every day of the year paint a mental picture of your life as you choose it to be.
**ISBN 0-932194-27-3** **$6.95**

*CHOICEMAKING: For Co-dependents, Adult Children and Spirituality Seekers* — Sharon Wegscheider-Cruse
This useful book defines the problems and solves them in a positive way.
**ISBN 0-932194-26-5** **$9.95**

*LEARNING TO LOVE YOURSELF: Finding Your Self-Worth*
Sharon Wegscheider-Cruse
"Self-worth is a choice, not a birthright", says the author as she shows us how we can choose positive self-esteem.
**ISBN 0-932194-39-7** **$7.95**

*BRADSHAW ON: THE FAMILY: A Revolutionary Way of Self-Discovery*
John Bradshaw
The host of the nationally televised series of the same name shows us how families can be healed and individuals can realize full potential.
**ISBN 0-932194-54-0** **$9.95**

*HEALING THE CHILD WITHIN:*
*Discovery and Recovery for Adult Children of Dysfunctional Families*
Charles Whitfield
Dr. Whitfield defines, describes and discovers how we can reach our Child Within to heal and nurture our woundedness.
**ISBN 0-932194-40-0** **$8.95**

Enterprise Center, 3201 S.W. 15th Street,
Deerfield Beach, FL 33442
1-800-851-9100

# *Daily Affirmation Books from . . . Health Communications*

*GENTLE REMINDERS FOR CO-DEPENDENTS: Daily Affirmations*
Mitzi Chandler
With insight and humor, Mitzi Chandler takes the co-dependent and the adult child through the year. Gentle Reminders is for those in recovery who seek to enjoy the miracle each day brings.
**ISBN 1-55874-020-1** **$6.95**

*TIME FOR JOY: Daily Affirmations*
Ruth Fishel
With quotations, thoughts and healing energizing affirmations these daily messages address the fears and imperfections of being human, guiding us through self-acceptance to a tangible peace and the place within where there is *time for joy.*
**ISBN 0-932194-82-6** **$6.95**

*CRY HOPE: Positive Affirmations For Healthy Living*
Jan Veltman
This book gives positive daily affirmations for seekers and those in recovery. Everyday is a new adventure, and change is a challenge.
**ISBN 0-932194-74-5** **$6.95**

*SAY YES TO LIFE: Daily Affirmations For Recovery*
Father Leo Booth
These meditations take you through the year day by day with Father Leo Booth, looking for answers and sometimes discovering that there are none. Father Leo tells us, "For the recovering compulsive person God is too important to miss — may you find Him now."
**IBN 0-932194-46-X** **$6.95**

*DAILY AFFIRMATIONS: For Adult Children of Alcoholics*
Rokelle Lerner
Affirmations are a way to discover personal awareness, growth and spiritual potential, and self-regard. Reading this book gives us an opportunity to nurture ourselves, learn who we are and what we want to become.
**ISBN 0-932194-47-3**
**(Little Red Book)** **$6.95**
**(New Cover Edition)** **$6.95**

Enterprise Center, 3201 S.W. 15th Street,
Deerfield Beach, FL 33442
1-800-851-9100

Health Communications, Inc.

# *Helpful 12-Step Books from . . . Health Communications*

*HEALING A BROKEN HEART:*
*12 Steps of Recovery for Adult Children*
Kathleen W.

This useful 12-Step book is presently the number one resource for all Adult Children support groups.

**ISBN 0-932194-65-6** **$7.95**

*12 STEPS TO SELF-PARENTING For Adult Children*
Philip Oliver-Diaz and Patricia A. O'Gorman

This gentle 12-Step guide takes the reader from pain to healing and self-parenting, from anger to forgiveness, and from fear and despair to recovery.

**ISBN 0-932194-68-0** **$7.95**

*THE 12-STEP STORY BOOKLETS*
Mary M. McKee

Each beautifully illustrated booklet deals with a step, using a story from nature in parable form. The 12 booklets (one for each step) lead us to a better understanding of ourselves and our recovery.

**ISBN 1-55874-002-3** **$8.95**

*WITH GENTLENESS, HUMOR AND LOVE:*
*A 12-Step Guide for Adult Children in Recovery*
Kathleen W. and Jewell E.

Focusing on adult child issues such as reparenting the inner child, self-esteem, intimacy and feelings, this well-organized workbook teaches techniques and tools for the 12-step recovery programs.

**ISBN 0-932194-77-X** **$7.95**

*GIFTS FOR PERSONAL GROWTH & RECOVERY*
Wayne Kritsberg

A goldmine of positive techniques for recovery (affirmations, journal writing, visualizations, guided meditations, etc.), this book is indispensable for those seeking personal growth.

**ISBN 0-932194-60-5** **$6.95**